Child by Child

Praise for *Child by Child*

The reader will be impressed by the book's organization, attention to details, and clarity of information. Parents, in particular, will benefit from the summaries of each exceptionality and their association with church programming. Church personnel will reference this book for strategies to nurture their communication and teaching abilities. I heartily recommend this innovative book for readers interested in servicing children with special needs in pursuit of their Christian education.

—Donald F. Perras, Ph.D., Professor of Special Education,
Southern Connecticut State University, New Haven, CT

Life is journey. Faith is journey. We live and learn in relationship with God, God's earth, and God's people. Child by child, step by step, with intention and attention, this manual is a guide to meeting, greeting, adapting, teaching, and worshipping together, with helpful strategies for everyone from the usher to the pastor, with loads of resources referenced for more specifics. For those just beginning the journey of inclusive ministries, or those already on the road, it's a map for action and reflection.

—Bill Gaventa, M.Div., The Elizabeth M. Boggs
Center on Developmental Disabilities UMDNJ
Robert Wood Johnson Medical School, New Brunswick, NJ

Susan's emphasis on forming relationships and building from an incarnational center makes an important theological statement about the way that we function as the Body of Christ. *Child by Child* moves us away from simply accommodating special needs to a place of honoring all individuals and naming gifts. This is an important contribution to the field of practical theology and makes contact with the whole Body: parents, children, teachers, clergy, and parishioners. Every church library would be smart to include this on their shelves!

—The Rev. Dr. Audrey Scanlan, Canon for Mission Collaboration,
Diocese of CT and Co-Director of "Rhythms of Grace."

Something (the Spirit?) has prompted Susan to stretch beyond her own experience to explore and reflect on the experience of children and parents facing developmental and learning challenges. She reports on extensive, patient reading in the particular patterns, dilemmas, challenges, and strengths that come to children and to families with very specific, clinically and educationally defined challenges, and she teaches herself and our communities to ask, "how do we make our intention to welcome all real in this instance?" Susan's compassionate reflection and inquiry guides her and us to specific practice choices any congregation can make to prepare itself for a welcome to strangers that may also help us discover the unspoken, hidden challenges families and children already active in the congregation are facing.

—The Reverend Donald Schell, President of All Saints Company
and co-founder of St. Gregory of Nyssa Episcopal Church, San Francisco

See more at www.churchpublishing.org/childbychild

Child by Child:

Supporting Children with
Learning Differences and Their Families

Susan Richardson

Morehouse Publishing
NEW YORK · HARRISBURG · DENVER

Morehouse Publishing, 4775 Linglestown Road, Harrisburg, PA 17112
Morehouse Publishing, 445 Fifth Avenue, New York, NY 10016
Morehouse Publishing is an imprint of Church Publishing Incorporated.

www.churchpublishing.org

Cover design by Laurie Klein Westhafer
Typeset by Denise Hoff

Library of Congress Cataloging-in-Publication Data

Richardson, Susan.
  Child by child : supporting children with learning differences and their
families / Susan Richardson.
      p. cm.
  Includes bibliographical references (p. 93) and index.
  ISBN 978-0-8192-2751-5 (pbk.) -- ISBN 978-0-8192-2752-2 (ebook)
1. Church work with learning disabled children. 2. Church work with
exceptional children. 3. Church work with learning disabled youth.
4. Christian education of children. 5. Christian education of teenagers.
6. Church work with families. I. Title.
  BV4461.R54 2011
  259'.43083--dc23
                              2011024696

Printed in the United States of America

With thanks
to the Episcopal Church Foundation
and
to Christ Church Philadelphia

871

Contents

❖

Acknowledgment

◈

My profound gratitude goes to the Episcopal Church Foundation and its staff and board; without their support and encouragement of me as an ECF Fellow, this guide simply would never have been written.

The clergy and people of Christ Church Philadelphia helped me, as their Assistant Minister, to birth and shape the project through that parish's unrelenting belief in connecting with the world, under the guidance of my rector and friend, the Reverend Timothy Safford. And then the people and staff of Grace-St. Paul's Church, Mercerville, New Jersey, took me on as rector.

Barbara Newman, William Gaventa, Erik Carter, and Don Perras have been invaluable in bringing to this project their knowledge, experience, and fervent dedication to a church that says "no" to no one. The CLC Network, in particular, contributed the expertise for the section on specific learning differences.

I'm grateful to my editor and encourager, Sharon Pearson, who helped me turn this from computer documents into something the world might actually find useful, and to the Reverend Stephanie Spellers, who inspires me toward an ever more radical welcome. My friend the Reverend Tom Brackett, missioner with the Episcopal Church, has a joyful and unceasing way of finding an open and exciting door where my brain doesn't even see a door at all and helping me truly believe that every step is to be celebrated. Sr. Rita Woehlcke, SSJ, continues to call me to a God who is always closer and more wonderful than my humanness can hold on to; thank goodness God holds on to me.

Loving gratitude to Linda and Zig Roebuck, who inspire and encourage me and have fun while doing it—back at ya! And finally, thanks to my son, Luke, for his patience, integrity, gentle heart, and a sense of humor that always puts things into the right perspective.

Introduction

❦

"Train children in the right way, and when old, they will not stray" reads the New Revised Standard Version translation of Proverbs 22:6. Other English translations may put it in slightly different ways, and all are useful.

But if we open up the Hebrew wording itself in all its richness and sensuality, we find the guiding principle that underlies *Child By Child*. The original Hebrew could easily read more like this: "Consecrate each child according to his own journey." The verb קֹדֶשׁ ([ch] ah n o [ch]) carries rich layers of meaning: to teach or train, but also to dedicate or consecrate. And we are to consecrate our children, each according to her particular way—in other words, her unique journey, path, or manner. His way. Her way. Nor our way.

Here we find our biblical mandate for supporting children and teens in our faith communities. Not by beginning with the program, event, or lesson, as important as those things are, but by beginning with the human being and his way, her path, his manner. By meeting them there, we then consecrate them, affirming their blessedness as people and claiming for and with them the holiness of the particular road their life will turn out to follow.

Indeed this vulnerability to someone's human particulars is also part of the biblical witness. Hospitality—far more fundamental to the ancient Israelites and to the Jews of Jesus' day than it is to us—requires that vulnerability to who someone uniquely is, to his or her ways of learning and being. As the stories of Abraham, Martha and Mary, and many others show in different ways, we are called by God to be vulnerable in our hospitality; to be changed by the nature of divinity revealed by those who come to the doors of our household.

Yet their divinity doesn't exist apart from their humanity. And those whose ministry it is to help build family programs in congregations know that there is no abstract "family." Each one comes with its story, gifts, and struggles, and as statistics suggest that approximately one in four families is affected by someone with a learning difference, many families come with that experience as part of their story. Like each of us, those families and their children want to be welcomed, known, and valued for who they are—not who they're not. And that means understanding differences and supporting individuals to the best of our ability, toward their full integration into the household of God.

Yet so many of us working in faith communities, whether lay or ordained, do not come to the job with background in special education or psychology. We may feel uncertain, unclear, or anxious about what to do. It's not that we are any less able to offer that support; we just need encouragement and help in doing it. The fact that we are not specialists need not keep us from embodying God's love to those who may especially need to believe in it.

Child By Child is an effort to create a map by which those working with children and teens with learning differences and their parents can find help with different aspects of welcoming them into the "household" and being changed by what they tell us about the divine, what we assume about God. You may need help developing a plan for integrating a family into the church programs, creating childcare alternatives at a parish event, supporting both paid and volunteer staff, or integrating a child or teen into particular Sunday School lessons. The hope is that this guide can be a partner in that process, point you to further references and resources, and be a helpful part of a journey that neither begins nor ends with a printed publication but with a human being.

Toward that end, *Child By Child* focuses on community support of children and teens with learning differences. There are many ways that people are physically challenged as well, and those physical differences sometimes, though not always, overlap with learning differences. The focus of this publication is a range of the most common learning differences, including dyslexia, attention deficit hyperactivity disorder (ADHD), autism spectrum disorder, and giftedness, among others.

Understanding the particular traits associated with any learning difference or disability is only one part of helping someone find her place in a congregation. We need to attend to the areas of need while at the same time inviting the people with those needs into a larger experience of inclusion. Not in a way that silently suggests that we're working to make an exception out of the kindness of our hearts, but in a way that acknowledges that we all need supports, we all have differences, we all fear inability, we all want to show our ability—and we're all in this together. As theologian Hans S. Reinders wrote of Jean Vanier, founder of the L'Arche communities for those with developmental disabilities, "There is no way of doing something for other people if you do not first learn how to receive whatever gift they have to offer, which presupposes your willingness to accept that you also are a person in need." (Reinders, ed., *Paradox of Disability*, p. 4).

Faith communities are the one place set up to affirm that most basic human need of simply *knowing we belong*. Whose are we? We're God's, and where we're going to experience that is in community. We can be told that over and over—but as any child can attest, true learning comes when we get to experience something for ourselves.

1

Begin: With People

In recent decades, there has been an important paradigm change in caring for people with differences and disabilities that, as a church, we need to be part of—and, ideally, leading. Since the 1970s, there has been a shift away from a "rules and regulations" approach to diagnosing and treating someone's condition to a person-centered approach, which takes the human being as a point of departure and then asks about that person's abilities as well as disabilities, strengths as well as challenges. This people-centered approach looks at how that person can best fit into a network or community of care, which, though involving professionals, uses people from across that person's daily life to form a unique web around him or her.

The shift from an institutional to an individual lens also brought to the fore the difference between seeing a disability as inherent in the person himself, and the disability as occurring where he interfaces with his context. A difference may, in itself, be an impairment or an atypical development that only becomes a "disability" when someone's environment doesn't match her ability or when we ourselves give it that judgment. (See Chapter 8 on the theology of difference and disability.)

While an institutional approach begins with "You don't fit," the relationship approach begins with "We can figure this out." Increasingly, faith communities that have embodied this shift focus first on relationships with children and the creation of a person-centered network around them and their families, and only then on programs. In these communities, programs, whether large or small, emerge from the cultivation of relationships with real people in real churches.

The "figure-out" approach is especially helpful when leadership is starting from scratch and does not yet have many resources in place. It allows for process, mistakes, change, and simply getting started when we otherwise might feel overwhelmed. Most important, it allows for a working environment in which judgmentalism— about either individuals or our own efforts at learning how to support them—is suspended.

A person-centered, relationship-building approach happens on several levels, all of which take time, patience—and lots of good humor:

Welcome!

- When new parents come in with a child, have teachers ask routinely, in a matter-of-fact way, what the child's areas of challenge and strength are or if s/he has a learning difference that the parent knows of. Share the information with the appropriate staff and clergy supervisor.

- Ask all parents, regardless of whether their children seem to have a learning difference, to fill out a form that includes a space for special concerns, areas of strength and challenge, and whether they'd like to talk confidentially with staff or clergy. [See Bibliography, CLC Network (*G.L.U.E.*), p. 96 for sample.]

- In the welcome material for all parents, include a specific paragraph, such as "We believe that every child is uniquely loved by God. We welcome children and teens with different learning styles and abilities, and are committed to integrating them and their families into our church programs. To help us, please include information about your child's needs in the written registration form and in conversation with his or her teacher and with clergy."

- Begin with the child's strengths and areas of comfort. So many systems ask parents to begin with their child or teen's deficits; faith communities need to view every child first in terms of his gifts.

- When meeting any child, but especially one with a clear difference, use person-centered language. Ask their name first, then ask them or their parents about themselves, such as: "Tell me about what he likes," or "Tell me about her concerns or sensitivities, or things we should avoid," being careful to use the child's name ("Tell me what John finds upsetting/helpful in the

classroom," or "What does Maria like to show she can do?").
Remember that other children will most likely copy the language
that you model for them.

- Ask how you can best support their child. Listen carefully—
parents know their kids best—for what they say is appropriate or
works well, and what are the more volatile, unpredictable areas,
such as mood swings; what the child tends to react to; or the
child's usual social style.

- Have images in the classroom that suggest inclusivity, such as
photos and drawings that include children with Down syndrome
or visual or hearing aids; physical accessibility assists also promote
inclusiveness.

Go Deeper with Parents

- Help parents understand that
you seek to create a partnership
with them; help them experience
their relationship with you in
that way.

- As parents talk to you about their
child, emphasize that you will
honor their confidentiality and ask
permission to share information.
Invite them to say only what
they are comfortable sharing.
(See sidebar for further suggested
questions.)

- If they'd like to share more about
their child, ask what they've learned
through their school experiences,
including through professional
evaluations, assessments, or
Individualized Education Programs
(IEPs). For instance, what works
well for this child (classroom
pacing, environment, etc.)? Offer,
but don't push, for them to share a
written assessment for confidential
use by the staff.

**Examples of additional
questions to ask parents:**

« What are ways your child would
enjoy being involved in parish life?

« What have her church experiences
been like in the past? Did she have
fears or hopes in coming to this
congregation?

« Describe your child's faith. How does
he think about God? How does his
faith grow best?

« What are your own hopes for your
child in this faith community? What
would help make coming to the
church—at any time of the week—
something she looks forward to?

« How can we help and support you,
as a parent?

For further suggestions, see Newman,
*Helping Kids Include Kids with
Disabilities*, p. 20.

- Ask whether (and how) the child and parents want the child's difference talked about by other staff, parents, and children. How does the child or teen understand his own diagnosis? Where is the family in terms of wanting it to be known? Responses can vary widely, from a strong preference that it not be mentioned at all to relief that you would support them in helping share the information and educate others in the faith community.

- When you refer to the child or teen, use "people-first" language, such as: "Jim has an intellectual disability (diagnosis)," not "Jim is mentally retarded." Or "Sarah has Down syndrome (or a diagnosis of Down syndrome)," not "Sarah is Down's." Or "Pablo communicates with his eyes (or device, etc.)," not "Pablo is nonverbal."

- Invite parents to meet with clergy or staff to share their concerns. Ask for a separate time and space for the meeting ("Sunday mornings are crazy for me, so let's set up a time when I can really listen to you"), and let that reflect to the parents the importance you place on them and the meeting.

- Emphasize regular attendance to parents. Regular participation in church programs for all children and teens significantly affects their ability to establish trusting, reliable relationships with caregivers, teachers, clergy, and peers. Being there infrequently makes it harder for kids, especially those with learning differences or disabilities, to adjust and form relationships. At the same time, be aware that even people who seem to come infrequently may still consider you to be "their church" as much as those who attend more often. Even if you feel you don't have a track record with each other, they may still come forward with a need or expectation.

- The younger the age at which kids are introduced into a program, the more thoroughly they get to know the setting, peers, and teachers, and the better others can get to know them. Again, relationship really only happens through face-time.

- Don't forget that giftedness or acceleration is also a learning difference and can exist alongside another difference in the same child. Sometimes children or teens who are gifted need even more special attention than others, so include that in the range of needs and differences you ask parents about. Inclusion of giftedness as an issue also helps level the playing field to avoid the idea of problems and instead focuses on differences, which we all have.

- Develop a support group for parents. How you do this depends on your context, but be careful not to think of it as just for parents of kids with more extreme needs. Many parents may feel they need support for any number of things they are dealing with at the moment, yet may be reluctant to come forward. Depending on your sense of your families, such a group can begin like a general faith and parenting series. You can begin with a topic that is specific to kids with learning differences, or alternatively, a topic that has broader applicability and can serve as an umbrella under which learning differences can fall. For instance, a series on being your child's advocate—an experience virtually all parents share— can begin with what parents have in common, developing deeper relationships and community support for particular needs within that topic.

- Be aware that parents of kids with learning differences have most likely already experienced rejection, possibly from churches, as well as suspicion, blame, and pain at seeing their child feel rejected or excluded. Be open to their stories and remain non-defensive. Say something like, "That sounds so painful; I hope it will be very different for you here. How can we work together to make that happen?"

- Allowing for humor about the child or the difference is fine—it's a normal and healthy way that families deal with challenges. Just be sure to follow the parent's lead.

Make a Plan

- For parents who have begun to partner with you around their child's strengths and challenges, work with them to establish a plan for the child and the family in your specific parish—often called a Religious Inclusion Plan or Christian Formation Plan. Have as your goal the inclusion of the child in a way that is meaningful to her and supportive of her parents as their needs change over time.

- Depending on the parents' willingness, the planning team should ideally include clergy and staff leaders who will be working with the child, and any adult helper who may work with the child.

- Published materials that provide helpful templates for the steps of creating a Christian Formation Plan include the G.L.U.E. manual (CLC Network); Newman, *Helping Kids Include Kids with Disabilities*, p. 21; Carter, pp. 100–101.

- Whether using a published guide or creating your own, consider these questions:
  - What is the child's learning style? What ways does he learn best, what ways create barriers for him, what areas are still unclear and in the process of being understood by the family and other professionals? What classroom strategies work best for this child? What strategies are ineffective?
  - Does the child need any physical assists?
  - In what ways is the child most likely to participate in the faith community—either on Sunday mornings or at other church events—at this stage in her life? Be explicit about the fact that those ways will most likely change over time, and the team needs to look for things that may be more satisfying for her in the future.
  - What is most important for the child in terms of experiencing a loving God and inclusion in God's household? How can those ideas be communicated through activities in the congregation?
  - Who are possible faith partners? Other church members who may not be teachers or supervisors may be helpful in other ways, such as sitting with the child during a service, reading to him during an event, or simply being on hand if the parent needs to tend to another child or go to the restroom.
  - In what ways do the parents need help or support? Referrals in the community, a parent group at the church, or particular parents to talk to who have children with similar issues can be helpful.
  - How can clergy work with parents to write their family's "history"—the stories around the child or children and what they wish for their next steps?
- Write it up: The final result can be written in a brief document with bullet points or areas for short-term steps and long-term goals in education, worship, justice work, and events. Give copies to the parents and other team members, and keep a copy in a confidential pastoral file. Have staff and clergy stay in dialogue with parents about how the plan seems to be going, and remain open and flexible to adapting it when something doesn't seem to work. Remember—anything you try is simply a great chance

to learn! Reconvene the team to update the plan as parents and teachers see the need.

- Remember that most important is the deepened relationship of trust and collaboration that the planning process encourages among the parents and staff.

But We Don't Have Anyone with Learning Differences Here!

Statistics suggest that a learning difference or disability, whether in the nuclear or extended family, impacts one in four families. The fact that it may not have been visible in your congregation may mean that church leadership hasn't yet named the issue in an ongoing way and in an atmosphere of openness, nonjudgmentalism, and flexibility. By cultivating a culture of acceptance, you may find more people coming forward with their stories and need for support. Indeed, some congregations cite inclusive education and worship as a key reason for church growth, both numerical and spiritual.

2

Embody: Atmosphere and Vision

I recently held a Sunday forum for parents, asking them the question, "When have you, or your child, felt excluded or unwelcome somewhere? What made a difference one way or the other?" I fully expected the answers to be about churches, including our own, or schools, or other institutions, and I was hoping to pick their brains for ways to get better at helping parents feel a connection. But as usual, things didn't go as I expected.

The number one situation in which children have felt excluded? Birthday parties. So instead of trying to steer the discussion back to my own self-interests of how to train Sunday School teachers or put out better PR materials, I just listened. And I think I still found the answers I was looking for, only not in terms of church logistics. The answer lay more in the atmosphere and real intentions of those who do the welcoming, whether it's a birthday party, a theme park, or a church.

Hospitality—in the deepest sense of a welcome that is challenging to the host, doesn't edit the guest, but does change the church—is a high priority in the church these days. Writers and speakers challenge us to look within ourselves and our congregations to question how deep welcoming the stranger truly goes, how much it means giving up control instead of commandeering it, and how well we understand welcome as not being about coffee hour. For example, the Reverend Stephanie

Spellers, in her book *Radical Welcome: Embracing God, the Other, and the Spirit of Transformation* (Church Publishing, 2006), brings together the theological and practical questions of who is being excluded within a congregation, even inadvertently—whom don't you see—and what the reasons for that might be. She offers a process that can guide a congregation through those questions in the real context—not an imagined one—in which they find themselves.

When you ask the question of whom you may be excluding in your own faith community, where in your answer are families with kids with learning differences? Are those families and children present, supported, and feel their differences can be named without setting them apart? Or are you like one priest I spoke to who said, "We have a Down's kid, but we don't have anybody with learning differences"? (And he wasn't being theological.)

To recall the statistics on families with a child with a learning difference—around one in four families affected either in the nuclear or the extended family—it's most likely that the people are present but do not yet feel comfortable bringing that part of their stories—of their challenges, grief, successes, and joys—explicitly into the congregation's life. How can we change that?

While the support of Sunday School teachers and clergy is important, it's not enough. Whether or not members are aware of it, a congregation inevitably embodies and projects a certain orientation or atmosphere. But awareness and intentionality around what atmosphere you want to create makes all the difference in what that atmosphere is like. If you're not intentional about what you do want to say, you may end up accidentally saying things you don't intend.

Do parents sense a space of fear, discomfort, lack of information, and even implicit judgmentalism? Or is what they encounter one of flexibility, relationship, openness to learning, and the chance to see all of us as having both abilities and inabilities?

Reflecting on Your Congregation's Culture

- What's the real on-the-ground atmosphere right now on inclusion in general? Is it a selective or passive inclusivity, or is it active, self-examining, and intentional? Does it challenge the congregation on a weekly basis in the way they go about all the ministries of the church? What's the approach in each of these areas on difference/disability in particular? How has it been named and accommodated so far? You may find the answers inevitably reflect something of how the congregation sees its work in social justice in general.

- When possible, talk to those families who have left the community or remain at its edges. What needs do they have, what's up in their lives? The answers may help them express the fears or frustration they have about becoming more known and involved.

- Is the congregation in a time of transition? Is it a time of question asking and interviewing? If so, what are people trying to be more open to, where are they feeling led?

- What are the questions or issues that come up in that transition? For instance, do people worry about including kids in church (either pro or con), do teachers feel frustrated or fearful around kids with differences, and are clergy oblivious or passive toward those families?

- If you happen to be in the process of writing a congregational profile, it's a good time to do some additional polling about accessibility and welcome, including specific ministries around property, program, and worship.

How Welcoming Are We?

« *Who's thinking about it?* Who has been part of the assessment process, especially regarding children and teens with learning differences? Clergy, teachers, other staff, church leadership, parents of children with differences, teens with learning differences, specialists from both inside and outside the congregation can all play a part.

« *What's happened so far?* You may have done more than you realize. Brainstorm with your team about how people have reached and connected with kids and families with learning differences. What steps have you taken intentionally together? Name and validate what's already been done.

« *What experiences are kids with learning differences having already?* Think about how they've already been integrated into Sunday School, youth group, church activities, justice work, and outings or retreats. Bring out observations of both what seems to be working, and what has not worked so well—without criticism or judgment.

« *What about kids who have no diagnosis* but aren't connecting easily with their peers or with group activities? How have you helped them find their comfort zones, talked to parents, and adapted materials? In other words, how are you welcoming all kids? Are there other groups of children—perhaps from different cultural, economic, or household backgrounds—who struggle to find their place in your congregation?

continued

« *How regularly and explicitly do staff planning, event logistics, and visioning* include adapting to children's differences?

« *How and how often are parents* either responding to staff questions about their children or asking questions of their own? How common is it for parents to talk about what they're working on or even struggling with regarding their children?

« *How are you getting the word out?* What have people done to reach beyond the known congregation to those at its edges and in the surrounding community? What are you doing to let other families in your broader community know that you want to welcome them—that there is a place for them in your church?

In the past year in your congregation, how often did you see kids with learning differences:

« Participating in worship

« Helping lead worship (acolytes, readers, etc.)

« In the music program

« Ushering or greeting

« Regularly attending Sunday School or youth group

« In kids' activities at larger parish events (and are there any adapted for kids with different sensitivities, such as sound sensitivity?)

« As a teen representative to vestry or other committees, task forces, or networks

« Involved in the congregation's justice work

« Talking to a teacher or clergyperson about school, home, or work

Transforming a Culture

Staff and Clergy

Church employees are crucial points of entry and relationship for families and children with learning differences. Information, support, and theological awareness need to be an ongoing part of the leadership's example within the faith community and with specific families. Much of this book is devoted to helping church leaders be responsive and attentive.

The Congregation

Be public and assertive about your congregation's efforts and intention to include those with learning differences. Be sure it's in announcements and program descriptions in the church bulletin, website, church e-mail lists, fliers, or postcards that you can hand to visitors or post in appropriate public places.

- Have a contact person, whether clergy or lay, for people in the congregation who have questions. That contact person needs to be someone who's good at listening and facilitating, understands confidentiality, and can liaison closely with other staff for referrals, pastoral information, and support. Have that person regularly update leadership within your congregation, such as vestry, elders, task forces or networks for families, and those who work on property or communications. He or she needs to be on-site on Sunday mornings as consistently as possible, to both embody and enable the parish's commitment to being available and responsive to children and teens with learning differences.

- Have clergy send an annual letter to parents in the congregation about the vision and theology (even if you don't call it theology) of welcoming all families, and the realistic ways they can experience that welcome. At times, including stewardship season, you could also include a letter or testimony from a parent whose child has learning differences and who has been able to work on it within the church.

- Use prayers and litanies within worship that name disability and difference; look for liturgical resources that are theologically sound, projecting a God who loves and does not blame, and who sees each of us as unique and beloved. Have family devotionals that include questions of difference available for parents to take home.

- Use varied and inclusive imagery in different locations throughout the meeting places of the congregation. For instance, photographs or drawings of people with differences as a natural part of a group, rather than the stained glass Jesus and stained glass children we still see so often. Include photos of the kids themselves (with parental permission and without including the child's full name). For example, take digital pictures of the kids in a group, cut the larger picture into jigsaw-puzzle pieces, then let the kids "put back together the church." Or take digital pictures and place them visually into a large church or other gathering space that the kids have drawn. Include these images in central gathering places for your congregation.

Faith Partners

They can be called different things: faith partners, helpers, or networks. But the idea is the same: linking the child or family who needs extra help with people throughout the congregation in ways that call forth different gifts for different situations. Perhaps a family is struggling to make it through diagnostic or special education paperwork for the first time, and there is someone in the congregation who knows that system well. Or a mom is having trouble getting a child with a disability to therapy during her working hours, and someone in the congregation is free to give that child a ride. Or a young boy is having trouble with reading, and a teacher in the congregation is up for some one-on-one work with that child, perhaps an empty nester who's great with young boys.

Enabling that process of connection can happen in different ways. It can be more informal as staff or clergy pair someone—a child or parent—with another member who'd like to be part of the process of welcoming and incorporating that family. That relationship can then grow as is appropriate to the two people.

Alternatively, staff and clergy can identify someone in the congregation who is gifted as a facilitator or guide who can help match specific needs a family has with other congregants' abilities, possibly in unexpected or unusual ways that arise from the needs and gifts that are present instead of from a predetermined format. First, the facilitator needs to be able to listen closely to the parents, learning about the child, the household, the history, and the needs they are currently facing. The facilitator then considers the congregation for people whose gifts, including the right timing to offer them, coincide with the family or child's needs—in other words, faith partners. The facilitator introduces the partners in a way that fosters relationship, whether in a small group, one-on-one meetings, or regular church events. Third, the facilitator helps the child or family bring their own gifts to the congregation, helping them find their own ministries. Then, perhaps most importantly, the facilitator bows out, leaving room for what becomes a circle of connections, as kids and parents feel they are empowered within a flow that lets them both receive and offer ministry.

The role of the facilitator can become more expansive, if he or she chooses to go through additional training, to connect with difference/disability networks within and beyond the congregation, and advocate actively within the congregation for increased awareness and education about differences and needs. For further discussion of this role, see a relatively early publication on this approach, *Supportive Care in the Congregation* (Dean A. Preheim-Bartel and Aldred H. Neufeldt, The Mennonite Central Committee 1986), and *Including People With Disabilities in Faith Communities* (Carter).

Finally, it's important to remember that connections can come through matching shared interests, as well as matching need and ability. Find people who share a gift, passion, or interest. Is there a kid who loves the Phillies, and a couple of adults who are Phillies fans? The relationship can begin on a more mutual level based on shared capacity, rather than on one as giver and the other as receiver.

In the Classroom

- If a child's learning difference is known and parents have given permission, help other kids within that child's age and stage learn comfort with her learning difference. If a child's difference is more obvious, other kids may ask questions, so ask the parents what kind of language or acknowledgement they want staff to use. Continue to lean toward person-centered language (not "John is retarded," but "John learns differently," or "John is intellectually challenged").

- Depending on the difference and how the family feels, with their permission teachers can send home information on a learning difference, such as autism, to the other classroom families. This option depends highly on the individual situation, but some parents find it helpful and relieving to have staff support them in being pro-active in educating the community and allowing the difference to be seen as a normal part of family and congregational life.

- Remember that overall, most kids will absorb and accept a child's difference more easily and less anxiously than adults will, especially if they've been in the congregation and programs together from a young age.

Kids Supporting Kids

Kids create their own community in the classroom and in congregational activities. They can become partners to each other and recognize each other's gifts in unique and perceptive ways. If a child with an area of difference shows especially unusual behavior, you may need to balance attending to that child with letting other kids voice their feelings about it, such as "Was something upsetting? Confusing?" Sometimes, with a kid's very visible difference, talking about it as a group is fine, as long as you've gotten a green light from the parent. One-on-one may be more appropriate for certain children in the room who are concerned or upset. Help kids know what roles they can and can't take. A peer who tends to try to be a "tutor" and instruct a child with learning differences about what to do and not do may need to be guided toward being a friend and all the special tasks that can include, instead of trying to fill the role of the teacher.

In addition to the faith partners described above, Sunday School teachers and youth leaders can create informal buddy systems for some children with differences. The child's difference need not be named explicitly, if parents haven't approved it or if it hasn't yet been part of the classroom community. But a peer who seems interested and able can be asked by the teacher to "Share Maria's book with her, and help her with words she doesn't know," or "Hold Max's hand when we walk together into the church."

A child or teen peer can become the leader in a circle around another child with a learning difference, particularly a more visible one. A child or teen with a learning difference who has abilities to help out another peer can become that person's "buddy." Those with learning differences not only need others to minister to them, but also need to discover ways they can minister to others.

Two resources particularly target helping kids understand and relate to peers who may seem different. *Helping Kids Include Kids with Disabilities* (Newman, 2001) offers specific lesson plans for helping a classroom understand and engage (1) how all our minds are different from each other, and (2) how kids with particular differences may learn or act in ways the others aren't used to. Again, with parents' permission, these lessons can be an effective way not just to say but also to experience that we're all different, but we're still all one in God. *Your Feet, My Shoes* (Bolt, 2009) lays out activities to help children in grades one through eight to engage peers with differences or disabilities.

Get the Welcoming Word Out

- In all your church materials, both online and on paper, regular and event-specific, be explicit about your congregation's welcome to all families and their differences.

- Include within your website and in a separate mailing a letter from clergy to parents emphasizing welcome, the theology and environment of the congregation, and the desire to know and understand their children. Then include a copy in future handouts to all new parents. Encourage parents whose children have had a good experience in your community to pass the word along to someone whose child has a learning difference or disability or to a network of such parents and caregivers.

- Reach out to local family counselors, psychologists, and school counselors to let them know about your program and your intention to include those with differences. They may be able to come and work with programs or parent groups in your church and may also, as they feel appropriate, refer to you people who are seeking a faith community.

It's a Process, Not a Task

It takes ongoing intentionality to focus a congregation in new ways on questions of difference or disability. If efforts are sporadic, unsupported by clergy and staff, and not integrated into the awareness and mission of the congregation, accommodating kids with differences can end up feeling ineffective and insurmountable. Raising awareness, building the program, and making any necessary physical/property changes or additions are all steps in the process, and they don't happen all at once. It's attitude before architecture; don't get trapped by money concerns right off the bat.

Keep integration at the forefront of your church's self-awareness—whether in the form of mission, program, justice work, or strategy—and remind yourself and others that what seem like mistakes, adjustments, or delays are valid parts of a congregation's learning, growth, and change. It's okay to make mistakes; the critical thing is to try to be intentional and simply give it your best effort. Including children and teens with learning differences and their families has to be lived out over time, during which a congregation takes increasing ownership and understanding of that part of their identity. The community's ability to acknowledge the underlying question, "Do we really believe you belong here, or are we just saying it?" and to answer "yes" will become evident in meeting challenges with flexibility and in commitment to these children over time.

3

Teach: Curricula

How a teen or child fits into a church program begins with him and his family and continues along many different pathways. But one of the main intersections of children, teachers, volunteers, clergy, and even visitors is still Sunday mornings—which, for kids, usually means Sunday School or youth group. And for teachers, that means the opportunity and challenges of integrating a classroom full of different personalities and learning styles into a lesson plan, most often drawn from an existing, published curriculum.

A range of curricula can be found in churches, and there are a number of well-known, tested, and theologically and educationally sound programs offered by denominational publishers. While we'll discuss here adapting materials for children, rather than the reverse, the reality is that your teachers have probably been adapting their materials for some time, making them work for the space, the size of the group, and the frequency of visitors, among other factors. This may simply be about supporting them more thoroughly as they adapt the materials to create even more fluid and effective Sunday morning experiences for children with learning differences.

Often, a child or teen may not have a clear or diagnosed learning difference. They may be in the process of being assessed; their parents may be in the early stages of determining if the behavior is part of a phase; or the child may simply be showing mild tendencies that are still within a range of what may be considered typical. All those situations are good reminders that the point is never the child's diagnostic label, but his or her strengths and needs. The adaptive suggestions below can be applied for kids in many situations.

Above all, remember—and remind your volunteers—that the goal is learning to practice faith, not perfection or correction of doctrine.

Integration

There are curricula available that segregate children and youth with severe learning differences from other classrooms. But the focus here is on adapting existing materials to include those children and teens. Whatever resources you have—even if only your best intentions, which are an excellent start—remember that, unless otherwise arrived at and stated by your leadership, the point is adapting the curriculum to the child, not trying to fix the child to meet the curriculum.

As you integrate any child, especially one with learning differences, into regular classroom meetings, begin with who and where the child is, with her strengths, weaknesses, sensitivities, and abilities. As much as possible, draw this information from steps taken in conversation or written information from parents, or from a plan developed by your team. But that's just a beginning—what's most important is an ongoing relationship with the child, conversation with the parents, lots of small steps, and trying one thing and then another, depending on what works as the child grows through different stages.

Choosing Your Curriculum

Choose your curriculum based on its range of skill types and support. It's important to choose one that incorporates flexibility with a range of learning styles and situations. But also be careful of the subtle, and sometimes not-so-subtle, theology that underlies any curriculum. Work with your clergy to be sure that the messages about who God is and who belongs to God are consistent with what your congregation seeks to embody. Selective inclusivity can give off warning signals to parents of children with differences or disabilities, and even subtle messages about a God who is anything other than loving, engaging, and challenging of human-made boundaries may not end up being very helpful to parents and children whose antennae are already finely tuned toward judgmentalism and rejection.

Workshops on choosing curricula, such as those available through Church Publishing Incorporated, can help, whenever it's possible for clergy, staff, or volunteers to attend. See also yearly updated charts of curricula and each one's style, requirements, skill sets, etc., such as those by Sharon Ely Pearson at Building Faith (http://www.buildfaith.org) or through the Center for the Ministry of Teaching (http://www.vts.edu/cmt) at Virginia Theological Seminary.

Adapting Your Lesson Plans

There are plenty of times teachers have to improvise on the spot. But as much as possible, adapting curriculum materials should take place in advance, to allow for balancing the goals of the lesson plan, the needs of the group, and the more salient needs of particular kids.

As for all our kids, be aware of including a range of learning possibilities in your teaching and lessons plans: group, individual, buddies; fine motor skills, larger motor skills; cognitive, imaginative; interactive, quiet; drama, craft, or music; and work stations, with different kinds of projects and materials.

Especially in smaller parishes where two, three, or more ages are combined in one class, have different activities ready for different ages or stages. Be aware of the different kinds of learning: cooperative learning, multiple intelligences, tactile/kinesthetic learning, auditory learning, and visual learning.

The less unstructured time there is in a Sunday School hour, the better. Structured down time or quiet time is a good and necessary part of a stimulating morning. But unstructured, unplanned, empty time—time between activities, while some kids complete a task, or while others are going to the bathroom or arriving or leaving—is more likely to cause anxiety or the need for redirection in children.

Remember that different kids learn at different paces anyway. A child with learning differences or disabilities may blend in with the group with no assistance. If assistance is needed, begin with the least obtrusive help, integrating your alternatives for the child as naturally as possible.

Remind yourself of the mantra—seek the child's strengths, while being aware of his or her limitations or growing edges. For example, if Sarah struggles with linear thinking, and the day's lesson plan involves talking with the group about an idea such as baptism or forgiveness, perhaps add to your plan an element of storytelling or imagining to demonstrate the definitions you're sharing. Those children who are excited by ideas can still engage you in thoughtful discussion, but Sarah and others have the alternative of imagining a story and then perhaps seeing what their imagination helps them comprehend. A concluding activity might be allowing the children to either write or draw what they think about baptism or forgiveness.

A suggested checklist in planning your lessons:

- What are the main activities planned in the lesson and how do you expect the class will realistically complete them?

- What is the biblical theme this lesson emphasizes, which can be repeated throughout the lesson in different ways?

- What children may have challenges and with which of the planned activities? What are their best ways of engaging the biblical idea from the lesson? If it helps, jot down a list of what they do and don't do well.

- How can you allow for a child to take extra time, while peers may be moving ahead?

> **For those who need an alternative:**
>
> « Can they do the activity, only with more time?
>
> « Can they do the activity, only with simpler goals?
>
> « Can they do the activity, but with different materials?
>
> « Can they do a different but similar activity, toward the same learning goal?
>
> « Do they need to work on a different task altogether, best suited to what they are comfortable doing?

Presenting the Lesson

- Use pictures and words for stories, as well as the expressions of your own face and hands.

- Give instructions both verbally and visually.

- When teaching ideas, be aware of the possibilities of using different senses: tactile (physical materials), verbal, auditory (including musical instruments and other objects that make sounds), visual (pictures, video, felt boards), and even smell (many biblical scenes and ideas involve the sense of smell and can be suggested by using things like oils, potpourri, and foods).

- Break projects down into several small steps in which a child can experience success, rather than as one or two goals at which, if they don't reach them, they can seem to "fail."

- Be sure to signal transitions that are coming up, using instructions such as: "Let's finish our story so we can begin to build our models," "As I get out the materials, be thinking about how you want to create your scene," or "It's time to stop, look, and listen."

Evaluate How It Went

A day or so after the class, think about how different children reacted to different activities, and take notes on each child. If a pattern occurs over time, it will help you to make your planning more effective and insightful.

Remember that whatever you learn in going deeper with one child or teen and his family will probably enhance your work with all the children in the group, either in insights into other children or in alternatives that the entire group enjoys. It's all learning, and it's all good!

In the Classroom

Know in advance what your lesson structure will be: opening activity (journal time, or going around the group, etc.); idea or story; craft or interaction; closure. As much as you can, have the classroom set up to reflect and accommodate the flow of events.

Set the tone in the classroom that each child is important and accepted—and different, each in his or her own way. Resources such as *Your Feet, My Shoes* or the *Inclusion Awareness Kit* (both from the CLC Network) give step-by-step guidelines for exercises that create awareness and acceptance for differences in general, as a natural and positive part of being human.

Bless play as well as the more structured ways of learning. Children learn through play. Their play is often how they engage ideas, but even more important, it's how they experience and are formed by their peers, formation that will help guide them and their parents to their next steps in faith. You can be intentional in incorporating playfulness and room for spontaneity in your lesson plan, and to allow play to emerge within the different activities, especially if there's time when you have children in different areas in the room. Teens will show their playfulness in different ways, including humor—which, again, needs to be both encouraged and guided toward appropriateness.

If you have professional teachers in your congregations, even if they don't volunteer to work with children, take time to seek their suggestions and help them be aware of that part of the community's life. This step is part of the circles/network strategy of developing wider and wider circles throughout the congregation so that people can use their gifts in different and flexible ways at different times. Teachers in the congregation may have good suggestions for interventions, craft projects, etc., even if they don't want to volunteer as a teacher on Sundays.

As much as you can, create special spaces in your gathering area that enable different kinds of experiences. For instance:

- A *quiet, less stimulating space.* Give it a name like "The Thinking Space" or "The Quiet Space," depending on age/stage of the children. When a child needs to spend time in a quiet space, avoid time-out language unless the child understands it as a clear disciplinary intervention and understands what the time-out is a consequence of. If it's simply that the child was over stimulated beyond her control and needed to refocus by spending time with another activity on her own, avoid having her or other children see it as punishment.

- An *action space.* Some children need a place to discharge physical energy. If it's possible in your setting, create an area where younger children can crawl through a tunnel, slide down a small plastic slide, or roll on a therapy ball at appropriate points in the gathering, such as at the opening or during a break. For teens, it may be walking around the church grounds or neighborhood, or physical activities like going bowling.

- A *library*, including books that appeal to a variety of ages and learning styles and emphasize inclusivity and difference.

- A *building area* that accommodates small-motor skills, such as cutting, pasting, drawing, assembling small model items, etc. This can be part of an *art center*, with a range of artistic materials.

- A *sensory area* can help children focus on tactile substances, like beans, water, sand, or squeezy balls. Be sure the materials are age-appropriate and do not pose a danger such as a choking hazard.

- Other possibilities include a *writing area* with different writing utensils and types of paper, and a *music or sonic center*, with instruments for making sounds as appropriate within the day's plan.

Use language with children that reinforces social relationships. For example, you can greet them by name, and you can also greet them as "friend." Refer to other children as friends when talking to the class ("Please be quiet, I can't hear what our friend Henry is saying."). Follow your congregation's culture in what you have the children call the teachers—whether by first name, a title and first name, a title and last name, etc.—but be consistent within a classroom. For teens, where programs often intentionally emphasize forming a mentoring relationship with the teachers, consider using first names, though again, church and personal preference are factors. If there's uncertainty, discuss this with your head pastor and supervisor to be sure that solutions are consistent with your culture and protocol.

Questions About Behavior

Have clear classroom boundaries that kids have helped to shape together, in ways that are age appropriate. Deciding the rules for "how we will be sure we hear our friends talk" will help everyone realize it's their ability to be heard that they're defending, too. Reinforce the boundaries consistently.

Some children, whether with learning differences or not, may have more trouble not saying hurtful things. Help model alternatives to them, such as "What you just said hurt my feelings, and we try not to hurt each other's feelings. If you don't like my shirt (hair, skin, etc.), can you tell me about something you do like?"

When needed, ask parents about the discipline strategies in their household. What behavior by the child is acceptable or unacceptable to the family? What interventions/consequences reinforce unacceptability? What forms of discipline/intervention does the child respond best to? For some children, you may need to work to understand how they realize they've done something wrong.

Redirection and Discipline

When there is a clear infraction of classroom rules, take the child aside to talk (never take them somewhere alone). Ask him if he understands what went wrong, what the consequences are of what he said or did (he dumped over the crayons and now everyone has to stop and clean them up), and what he could have done instead (he could have asked for help finding the green crayon). The questions will vary based on the child's age and learning style. For a child who doesn't understand what was "wrong" about the behavior, base your intervention on what you've worked out with her parents. If there is an incident between children, let the other parents know if their child was involved. Be aware that a child with exceptional needs may have been provoked with unkind behavior. When a child acts out, there could be many reasons: medical, escape or avoidance, the need for attention, or too much sensory stimulation.

If other kids join in bad behavior, use the same techniques with them, taking them aside, questioning them about it, and setting up alternatives and consequences. As always, document any physical assault between children, no matter how minor it seems; alert the supervisor and the parents.

Give instructions in the affirmative ("Remember to . . . "). Give only the alternatives that are acceptable, and think through the alternatives and reasons alongside the child, then follow through with the conclusions.

Above all, remember that relationship and communication take time to grow.

Previously Unnamed Issues

If you need to raise an issue that the parent hasn't brought up, give it language such as "I noticed John seems sensitive to . . . [light stimulus, noise] or challenged by . . . [understanding directions]. Can you help me understand more about that?" Then follow the parents' lead in opening up the topic. If you feel a parent is reluctant to talk about a perceived problem a child is having, let your clergy know so that they can incorporate that awareness into their pastoral oversight of that family and can also discern whether staff need additional support or education.

Small Steps Matter

Remember that for some kids, such as those intellectually challenged or further along on the autism spectrum, the goal isn't to grow by visible leaps and bounds. Begin with the child presented to you; get to know where they are. What seems like a small step can be huge, significant, and something to celebrate. Acknowledge any success as a victory for them and for their parents, though without praising them gratuitously as they may feel patronized or singled out. Often just naming a successful step is sufficient. As with all kids, they just need to feel seen and understood.

4

Understand: A Guide to Learning Differences

While it's important to remember that each individual is a mix of strength areas and areas of need, psychologists, doctors, and educational teams have terms and designations for some of these need and strength areas. A child with a high IQ, for example, might be known as "gifted and talented." A child with a particular pattern of social and behavioral differences might be known as having an "autism spectrum disorder." As a church, however, we must filter such terminology through our theology of a loving and inclusive God, and mysteries of exactly how God works that we can't always explain, all underlain by a belief that God is seeing us all in ways more deep and insightful than we can see ourselves and each other.

As clergy, teachers, and other congregants are getting to know a child and his family, it's helpful for them to know about some of the information associated with this child's unique pattern. That information can help us best equip our leaders and peers for a successful plan that allows us to embrace the child, use her gift areas to enrich others, and support her areas of need.

For each area listed, you will find a brief description of that designation, differences and characteristics of that category, possible interventions, and additional resources.

Attention Deficit/Hyperactivity Disorder (AD/HD)

Description:

One job of the brain is to help us attend to the tasks we do each day. The brain has chemicals that allow us to focus our attention on a task, control behavior, and keep the body still when needed. When these chemicals, or neurotransmitters, are not working as well as they could, a person is known as having AD/HD. There are three types of AD/HD: inattentive type, hyperactive-impulsive type, and combined type.

Characteristics:

AD/HD Inattentive Type. This child might find it difficult to:

- Focus on the Bible story, discussion, or other tasks
- Notice specific details, like following all three steps of the directions just given
- Organize supplies or materials, like remembering to get both a pencil and scissors for the activity time
- Follow through on short-term and long-term projects and tasks

AD/HD Hyperactive-Impulsive Type. This child might find it difficult to:

- Keep the body from fidgeting, squirming, and moving
- Stay seated during worship or small-group times
- Play quietly
- Wait to answer a question or take a turn without interrupting or blurting out an answer
- Think carefully about the consequences of an action, and act before thinking

AD/HD Combined Type. Some children have both sets of characteristics, showing signs of inattention as well as impulsivity.

Interventions:

1. Find ways to use this child's gifts as a way to engage him in the activities. A child gifted in drawing may want to illustrate the Bible story or text during the talking time. Another child with high energy and good coordination may be able to lead others in exercises to help everyone use up some excess energy. Other children with good visual skills may want to construct a model of the Temple from Legos or build using blocks to represent a portion of the story. A child gifted with

words might be able to put together a word search or cross-word puzzle to illustrate the concepts represented. Act out, build, move, stretch, construct. Think of additional verbs that could be associated with your time together at church, and match those to the child's gift areas. Let the child shine.

2. Give choices in seating and activities. Sometimes children are more successful in paying attention when there are movement options. Sitting on an exercise ball or a cushion filled with air might be enough movement beneath the child to allow her to better focus on your words. Allowing a child to complete an activity or listen while seated, standing, kneeling, or rocking in a rocking chair might also help him to focus on the task at hand.

3. Provide breaks as needed. Some children might appreciate carrying a box of books down to the church office or library as a way to help and get some extra movement. Running errands or doing short movements or exercises mixed inside lessons or worship can be very helpful.

4. Use visuals. Posting rules, directions, samples, and expectations allows children to have the boundaries and instructions always visible, even if the brain takes a short trip. The visual is always available to reference.

5. Be understanding. Some children may take medication to help support the brain chemicals that allow an individual to pay attention. Some of these medications, however, may be in the process of running out during evening hours. Some parents may choose to have children take medications only during the school week, but not on weekend days. Both of these situations can make evening church meetings and Sunday settings more challenging for a child with AD/HD.

6. Follow through on existing support. Children may find that certain pencils, weighted items, behavior charts, or timers can really help in the area of attention. Find out what works in other environments and see if those same things might be helpful when used in a church setting.

Resources:
1. *Learning Disabilities and the Church: Including All God's Kids in Your Education and Worship* by Cynthia Holder Rich and Martha Ross-Mockaitis (Faith Alive Christian Resources, 2006)

2. *Reaching for a New Potential: A Life Guide for Adults with ADD from a Fellow Traveler* by Oren Mason M.D. (2010)
3. *The ADHD Book of Lists* by Sandra R. Rief (Jossey-Bass, 2003)
4. Children and Adults with Attention Deficit/Hyperactive Disorder (CHADD), http://www.chadd.org/

Autism Spectrum Disorder (ASD)

Description:
Autism spectrum disorder is a neurological, or brain, difference. Children with ASD exhibit a wide spectrum of differences in language understanding, social skills, repetitive themes and behaviors, desire for routine, perspective-taking ability, and sensory responses.

Characteristics:
Remember, the word "spectrum" means that some children will demonstrate these differences in significant ways while others will show them in more mild ways.

Language Understanding
Children may:
- Be unable to use spoken words and may communicate through sign language or systems involving pictures or printed words
- Understand very few spoken words, sometimes hearing only a portion of the words in a sentence
- Understand words very literally, being surprised that it's "raining cats and dogs" or that someone would suggest you should "give your heart to Jesus"
- Hold one-sided conversations, not understanding the give and take among friends
- Have a hard time understanding your use of humor and the jokes and riddles their friends tell

Social Skills
Children may:
- Try to hide from or escape social settings
- Be confused with body language and facial expressions
- Make social errors or blunders, often not recognizing that their words or actions were inappropriate

- Incorrectly analyze the best course of action or direction in a social setting

Repetitive Themes and Behaviors
Children may:

- Have a great fascination with one topic, such as trains, a particular movie, or computers
- Repeat the same action, such as lining up toy cars or making sure each chair is sitting in exactly the correct spot, and may get upset when you make changes
- Be limited in the types of activities they enjoy

Desire for Routine
Children may:

- Seek to know the schedule, routine, or order of worship
- Get upset when that schedule is altered or suspended without advance warning in a way they will understand

Perspective-taking Ability
Children may:

- Know only their own perspective and advocate for their idea with great passion
- Find it hard to accurately know what others might be thinking, feeling, and experiencing, so it may be hard for them to predict or understand their friends' responses

Sensory Responses
Children may:

- Have one or more sensory systems that process information differently. Sounds might be very loud to one person while another child may need extra volume to penetrate the senses. One child may crave heavy, hard touch while another child might get hurt from someone brushing against him lightly.
- Have differences in the way they respond to sights, sounds, tastes, smells, touches, balance, and pressure

Interventions:

1. Get to know the individual child. Find out what activities that child really enjoys and what might be difficult. Find out especially what sensory differences the child has and what that will mean for your church setting.

2. Visual supports are very important. Vision is often a very stable sensory system, so using picture or word schedules, devising behavior systems using visual supports, and illustrating a biblical concept with pictures or real objects can often enhance communication.

3. Create a predictable schedule or routine. If that routine needs to be changed, give advance warning in a way that individual will understand (moving pictures around on a picture schedule, providing an alternate order of worship for the day).

4. Understand how that child interprets words. Telling a child who interprets words literally that they are "drinking the blood of Jesus," for example, can be a frightening thing. If a child can point to pictures, get some pictures. If a child knows some sign language, learn those signs. Try to avoid using too many words.

5. Allow peer groups to better understand that child by giving accurate, positive, and honest information about ASD.

Resources:

1. *Autism and Your Church* by Barbara J. Newman (Faith Alive Christian Resources and CLC Network, 2006)
2. *Autism and Your Church Training DVD* by Barbara J. Newman (CLC Network)
3. *Church Welcome Story* by CLC Network
4. *ASD to Z* by Laurel Hoekman (The Gray Center)
5. *Helping Kids Include Kids with Disabilities* by Barbara J. Newman (Faith Alive Christian Resources and CLC Network, 2001)
6. *Autism and Alleluias* by Kathleen Bolduc (Judson Press, 2010)

Behavioral/Emotional Disorders

Description:

Some words that psychologists and educators use describe several conditions under this heading. Whether it be anxiety disorders, bipolar disorder, conduct disorder, depression, or some other area related to behavior and emotions, children identified in this area will show these patterns over a long period of time and in such a way that interferes with daily life. School may be difficult. Home relationships might be a challenge. Friendships and feelings are disrupted. Children might withdraw or act out. They might be impulsive or full of fear.

Characteristics:

Anxiety Disorders

- Children experience excessive and intense levels of anxiety.
- These anxious feelings might be known as generalized anxiety disorder, obsessive-compulsive disorder, panic disorder, posttraumatic stress disorder, or social anxiety disorder.
- Children with obsessive-compulsive disorder may have uncontrollable urges to engage in certain rituals like excessive hand washing or may make repetitive body movements or noises.
- Whatever the more specific terms, children with anxiety disorders might show fear and frustration in a situation that would not be problematic for most children.
- The feelings of anxiety might seem overwhelming and uncontrollable to the child.
- Medications may be helpful and effective in treating anxiety disorders.

Bipolar Disorder

- Sometimes known as manic-depressive illness, bipolar disorder will cause a child to have sudden mood swings.
- On one end, a child might feel full of energy, irritable, or "high." On the other end, a child might feel hopeless and sad. While there are often times of stable mood somewhere in the middle, children can cycle rapidly between the highs and lows of mood. Children can also display some intense behaviors during both ends of this disorder.
- Medicine from physicians and therapy from psychologists may help support children with bipolar disorder.

Conduct Disorder

- Children who have a very difficult time following rules or behaving in socially acceptable ways might be known as having a conduct disorder. Children might be aggressive to people, animals, or property and may require additional adult supervision.

- Children might have ongoing patterns of lying, stealing, or breaking rules.
- While all children might lie, hit, or steal upon occasion, children with a conduct disorder show a significant pattern of these behaviors over time.
- Counselors and psychologists might work with the children but also with the parents in helping the children make better choices in the future.

Depression

- While we all experience times of sadness, a child with depression will experience persistent sadness, irritable mood, and loss of interest or pleasure in activities.
- Depression might limit a child's interest in eating, decrease her energy levels, shake her once positive self-image, and make her feel hopeless.
- Children with depression can't just "snap out of it." They may not want to sing the praise and worship songs. Songs of lament may more closely mirror their moods.
- Children with depression may consider options such as cutting themselves and talk of committing suicide. If you observe any dangerous behavior, you should stay with the child and contact his parents immediately.
- Medications may be effective in treating depression.

While this list of behavioral and emotional disorders is not complete, it's important to remember some of the diagnoses we often associate with adults can very much be part of the life of a child.

Interventions:

1. Refrain from placing judgment and blame on children and families. The causes and treatments are complex. The family will require your support and encouragement.
2. Arm yourself with information. So often, individuals feel they must hide issues related to mental health problems from other church members because they feel ashamed. Understand the brain chemicals and physical differences related to these issues. Understand the cautions and

symptoms so that you can have a trained pair of eyes on the individual.

3. Find out what supports and plans are in place for the child. What do you do if the child expresses anxiety or depression? What if a child suddenly gouges holes into tables and materials? How might you handle a child who refuses to come to church functions due to depression? While there are no easy answers to these specific questions to print in this guide, the overall answer is the same. Know the child, become familiar with the area of difference, and participate with parents and professionals in following an individualized plan for the child. Parents are a priceless resource.

4. Make accommodations and choices based on the child attending at the time. Mood disorders can be cyclical, so children may not be capable of performing consistently each week.

5. Hold on tightly to the promises in Jeremiah 29:11: "For surely I know the plans I have for you, says the Lord, plans for your welfare and not for harm, to give you a future with hope." Sometimes children and parents need you to hold on to this verse alongside of them as well as on their behalf. That hope and future can become obscured at times, and the gift of someone who can still see that place is without measure.

Resources:

1. American Academy of Child and Adolescent Psychiatry, http://aacap.org/page.ww?name=The+Depressed+Child&section=Facts+for+Families

2. Anxiety Disorders Association of America, http://www.adaa.org/living-with-anxiety/children

3. *Kids in the Syndrome Mix of ADHD, LD, Asperger's, Tourette's, Bipolar and More!: The One Stop Guide for Parents, Teachers, and Other Professionals* by Martin L. Kutscher, Robert R. Wolff, Tony Attwood (Jessica Kingsley Publishers, 2007)

Cerebral Palsy (CP)

Description:

"Cerebral" refers to the brain. "Palsy" refers to weakness in the muscles. Cerebral palsy describes a condition where injury to a portion of the brain makes areas of weakness in the muscles of the body. That injury to the brain can happen before birth, during the birth process, or soon after birth. CP can be mild, causing a child to appear clumsy at times. It can also be moderate, in which case a child might speak differently or have a noticeable difference in an arm or leg. When CP is severe, multiple areas of weakness are often present in the child's body, many times requiring supports such as wheelchairs, walkers, and alternate forms of communication.

Characteristics:

Descriptions of different types of CP usually talk about muscle tone as well as what parts of the body are involved.

Muscle Tone

Children may:

- Have muscles that are very tight, making movements in legs or arms look "stiff"
- Have muscles that often move or shake slowly without conscious control, with low muscle tone. This child may have difficulty sitting up or walking without support.
- Have muscles that are not well coordinated with the rest of the body, often impacting balance and visual perception
- Have all of these issues at the same time

Parts of the Body

Children may have differences in:

- Legs
- One side of the body
- Arms, legs, face, and body

Additional Issues

Some children with CP may have additional differences involving learning, vision, hearing, attention, or speaking. For some children, there are no additional areas of difference.

Interventions:

1. Become very familiar with the individual child. It's possible, for example, to have a child with typical intelligence who has voluntary muscle control over only one body part—blinking the eyes.

2. Understand any specialized equipment. Some children will use walkers, crutches, wheelchairs, or talking communication computers. Some children with more mild forms of CP may benefit from a specific type of pencil or scissors to be more successful. Know what this equipment is and incorporate these items into your church setting.

3. Learn about the ways you can support everyday tasks such as eating, drinking, using the bathroom, or getting on a coat. Some children will need assistance. By finding out exactly what is needed, you avoid the problems of offering too much or too little help.

4. Allow peers to be comfortable. By explaining the child's specialized equipment, walking differences, or uncontrolled movements, you can make the other children more comfortable. If a child uses a walker, try to get a second walker to allow the children to try it out. If the child uses a communication computer, teach the other children how it works so they can best interact.

5. Be creative. Think of ways the child can be involved with the materials and with peers, even if it's done a bit differently. Perhaps the child speaks the answer instead of writing it. Perhaps the child times the game that involves running. A child may be paired with a peer and they participate together. Get to know the child and then make the needed changes so she can be fully involved in the activities.

Resources

1. *Special Needs SMART Pages* by Joni & Friends (Gospel Light, 2009)
2. *Helping Kids Include Kids with Disabilities* by Barbara J. Newman (Faith Alive Christian Resources and CLC Network, 2001)
3. United Cerebral Palsy, http://www.ucp.org

Deafness, Hearing Loss

Description:

Whether it's due to genetics, disease, or trauma, some children struggle with hearing. The hearing loss they have may be considered mild, moderate, severe, or profound. Sometimes the hearing loss is only in one ear, and sometimes in both. Tests are done to find out the extent of the hearing loss as well as which sounds might be more difficult to hear. Some hearing losses are associated with higher pitches and others with lower ones. Ear surgery as well as hearing aids or other kinds of amplification can often help improve the child's hearing. A child is considered to have deafness when her hearing loss is greater than ninety decibels.

Characteristics:

A child with a hearing loss might:

- Frequently ask you to repeat something you have said
- Turn the volume up on many electronics
- Not respond to his name
- Have delays in speech sounds or talking

A child with a hearing aid or amplification system might:

- Appreciate a room without a lot of background noise
- Ask you to wear a special device that puts your voice directly into the ear without background noise
- Operate best if your large-group setting is equipped with an FM system or a setting that interacts directly with the hearing device

A child with deafness might:

- Use sign language to communicate
- Struggle to produce some speech sounds
- Read your lips to understand what you have said
- Also use an amplification system or have a cochlear implant

Interventions:

1. Find out about the child in your group and any equipment that might make church a better place to be.
2. Understand how to help the child should the equipment malfunction. Knowing where there are extra batteries and how to replace them can mean the difference between hearing well and hearing very little.
3. Find out what seating placement is best for a child. Perhaps one ear has better hearing than the other, and the child should sit with that ear towards the speaker. Another child may need to see your face as you talk, so placing that child directly in front of you would be important.

4. Loud noises, unexpected sounds, and even applause can be difficult for amplification systems to interpret. If the child looks confused, use your voice to tell the child what is happening or needs to happen next.

5. With the parent's permission, talk to the group about their friend and what might be the most helpful for that individual. It allows children to be better friends with one another.

Resources:

1. *Helping Kids Include Kids with Disabilities* by Barbara J. Newman (Faith Alive Christian Resources and CLC Network, 2001)

2. National Institute on Deafness and other Communication Disorders, http://www.nidcd.nih.gov/health/hearing/coch.asp

Epilepsy

Description:

While some children might have a seizure from a high fever or some other identifiable cause, when a child has two or more unprovoked seizures, that child is then known as having epilepsy. A seizure is caused when the brain has a brief surge of electrical signals. The seizure may impact a small portion or all parts of the brain. The episode might last for a few seconds or a few minutes. While a person in the room won't be able to see what is happening in the brain, one can often notice the impact that seizure has on the body. While there are many types of seizures, they basically fall into two larger categories: generalized seizures and partial seizures.

Characteristics:

Generalized Seizures

- This type involves both sides of the brain.

- One of the most common types is known as a "tonic clonic" seizure in which the child will lose consciousness, his arms and legs might stiffen, and then his body will begin to jerk. A child will most often sleep after the episode and will not remember what happened. These seizures often last for one to two minutes, and will require medical intervention if the seizure continues for longer than three minutes.

- Another common type of generalized seizure is called an "absence" seizure. These last anywhere from two to fifteen seconds and the person will usually stare off into space, unaware of the environment for a few seconds. Sometimes a child might blink or make chewing movements, and then resume whatever she was doing before the seizure. These often happen without any others noticing, and the child will not remember the seizure.

Partial Seizures

- Simple partial seizures happen when only one side of the brain is involved, and the child does not lose consciousness. The child's body might shake or the child may have odd sensations, but the child will be aware of the seizure activity.

- Complex partial seizures also involve only one portion of the brain, but the child does lose consciousness, or become less aware. Sometimes the child participates in a repetitive behavior that might even look like the child has control, but it is an unconscious behavior that the child usually does not remember afterward.

Interventions:

1. Know what to do if a seizure happens in your environment, and have the proper medical supplies available in an instant. Once a child has been diagnosed with epilepsy, there will be a protocol to follow that may differ among children. Make sure all leaders know what to do and how to intervene for each child.

2. If a child has a tonic clonic seizure when other children are present, it might be helpful to take the other children on a walk in the building so that other adults can attend to the child who is having the seizure. If there is a good chance the other children will see a seizure, it's important to explain to them about seizures and what they might see.

3. Think through your environment for safety issues. A child who loses consciousness, for example, should sit on the bottom row of the bleachers and avoid slides and jungle gyms. Work with parents to know what is and is not safe.

4. Have visuals available. Children coming in and out of seizures will need anchors to help them best understand what you have covered and what is expected of them. Posting visual samples, checklists, instructions, and schedules allows a child to reference what comes next.

5. Compensate for areas involving memory. Having a peer available to repeat instructions or recording important information or sessions allows a child to access the information at a different time.

Resources:

1. *Children With Seizures: A Guide for Parents, Teachers, and Other Professionals* by Martin L. and M.D. Kutscher (Jessica Kingsley Publishers, 2006)

2. *Epilepsy Explained: A Book for People Who Want to Know More* by Marcus Reuber, Christian E. Elger, and Steven C. Schachter (Oxford University Press, 2009)

3. Epilepsy Foundation, http://www.epilepsyfoundation.org

Intellectual Disabilities

Description:

Children with an intellectual disability (sometimes known as cognitive impairment or mental impairment) have limitations in areas connected with mental functioning. Areas such as academic skills, communication skills, self-care skills, and social skills will develop more slowly over time when compared to peers. It's important to remember, however, that children with intellectual disabilities are able to learn many concepts and skills, but it will often take a longer time and require a different approach.

Characteristics:

Mild to Severe

It's important to remember that some children may have a mild form of disability while others have a moderate or severe form. Psychologists will measure a child's IQ and pair that with information about daily functioning to determine the level from mild to severe. You may see only subtle, yet important, differences in those children with mild impairment. For those children with moderate to severe impairments, you will want lots of parent involvement in your planning.

Genetic Conditions

Some children with an intellectual disability have some sort of genetic difference. Children with Down syndrome, for example, are born with forty-seven chromosomes instead of forty-six. That genetic difference, present in every cell in the child's body, leads to developmental differences in both the body and the brain. A child's muscle tone, facial features, and skill development will be set according to the pattern of those forty-seven chromosomes. In addition to Down syndrome, there are many other genetic differences that can cause an intellectual disability. Additions and deletions anywhere in the chromosomal pattern will have some sort of impact on body and brain development.

Other Factors

In addition to genetic conditions, some children experience brain development differences before birth, during delivery, or from health concerns after birth. Cells may divide differently due to random factors, alcohol or drug use may result in developmental differences, the baby may not have adequate oxygen flow, or a child may be exposed to a disease or poison. Accidental injuries resulting in traumatic brain injury may also limit a child's intellectual ability. There are many possible causes for a child to have some sort of intellectual disability.

Gift Areas

It's important to remember that each person has a gift to bring to the body of Christ. That is certainly true for persons with intellectual disabilities. Remember to search out and use the areas of strength so that a child may serve as a greeter, a song leader, a prayer partner, an offering collector, or any area that is a good fit for this boy or girl.

Interventions:

1. Find out about the child's history. What activities and areas are easy for this person? What activities and areas are difficult? When you are planning your lesson or worship experience, think about how the child might be included and what might need to be changed or adapted.

2. Communication is really important. Some children might communicate with spoken words and others might supplement spoken words with sign language, pictures, or other speaking devices. It's important to know exactly how that child both gives and receives information so that you can make connections throughout your time together.

3. Be concrete. Present information with pictures, visuals, songs, and repeated phrases. Apply the lesson to very practical applications that will be meaningful to that child. You will soon discover that making the material and activities meaningful for this child will also pull other children into the topic in new ways.

4. Think about smaller pieces of a larger lesson or activity. If you cut out the figures of Moses and Aaron for the child, perhaps he can cut the straight lines for the house. If you write nine of the words, perhaps the child can trace over one of the words written in highlighter. If you ask four questions of the other children, perhaps you can ask, "Who was your favorite character in the story?" holding out two pictures for the child to choose from in giving an answer. Be creative. Think about what the child *can* do and make arrangements for the other portions.

5. Use buddies, helpers, volunteers, and peers. Sometimes it's helpful to have one person involved in the church setting who can step in and help out individually as needed. This person might be a partner in a larger group setting, or this person could use a portion of the time to instruct one-on-one with the child using alternate materials.

6. Be respectful of the child's age. While it might be tempting to treat that individual as a much younger person, don't do it. Adapt materials for the person's level of understanding, but sing songs, do activities, and have materials that best match the child's age. Try your best to include that child with others his or her age. Remember, inclusion is not only helpful for the individual; it's helpful for the rest of the group as well.

7. Get good instructions in areas such as behavioral expectations and self-care skills. It's important that you know how and when to help a child. Will that person need help in the bathroom? Does that individual have any choking or eating issues? What is helpful to do when a child chooses not to obey the adult in charge? Have all the volunteers working with this child know the answers to these questions. You will all need to know the plan and follow it to be the most successful.

Resources:

1. American Association on Intellectual and Developmental Disabilities, http://www.aaidd.org and http://www.aamr.org

2. Friendship Ministries, http://www.friendship.org

3. *The G.L.U.E Training Manual* by Kimberley Luurtsema and Barbara J. Newman (CLC Network, 2009)

Learning Disabilities

Description:

"Learning disabilities" is a large category that describes the challenges of children who typically have average intelligence, but also have some kind of difference in the way the brain takes in, processes, or gives out certain information. Academic skills including reading, writing, listening, speaking, or math may be affected. Sometimes only one area is impacted, sometimes multiple areas. A learning disability often shows up when a child is in elementary school. Despite good teaching and every expectation that a child will be successful, that child really struggles in one or more areas and might need some additional support in order to be successful at school.

Characteristics:

The School and Church Connection

Even though it is not the purpose of most churches to teach children to read, write, speak, and do math, many activities at church do involve these skill areas. Children are expected to write answers, listen and then give a verbal response, read a Scripture passage, or calculate the bowling score at a Youth Group function. When a child struggles in one of these areas at school, the issue will follow the child to church activities. For this reason, it's important that you know what areas are easy for the child and what areas might be difficult.

Those Struggling with Reading

Children may have a hard time learning to read, may have difficulty reading aloud, and may struggle to comprehend what they just read.

Those Struggling with Writing

Children may have difficulty spelling words, have a hard time holding a pencil, have messy handwriting, and struggle to write ideas on paper. They may spend a lot of time scratching through or erasing their work.

Those Struggling with Listening and Speaking

Children may speak later than expected, have limited vocabulary, have difficulty hearing what letter sounds make up words, have a difficult time hearing the differences between words, struggle to tell a story, struggle to understand jokes and sarcasm, mispronounce words, struggle to follow spoken directions, and have difficulty organizing thoughts to produce an answer to a question.

Those Struggling with Math

Children may confuse math symbols or misread numbers, struggle with math computation, struggle to help count the collection or make change, and misunderstand stories that involve numbers.

Children with learning disabilities are usually smart, trying their hardest, and want to be successful. They should never be thought of as lazy, slow, or unmotivated.

Interventions:

1. Get to know the child and what areas are strengths and what areas are difficult. Remember to offer opportunities each week for the child to demonstrate her areas of strength.

2. Get to know the child's areas of struggle and what supports might be helpful. If the child uses a certain pencil at school, get one for church. If the child uses a laptop for writing, have that come to church as well if there is a writing task. If the child often has someone read aloud to him, make sure that support is available at church. Most of the time, there are items or methods that can allow a child to participate.

3. Never embarrass a child by forcing her to display the weaker area in front of peers. For example, if a child struggles to recite Bible verses from memory aloud in front of others, perhaps writing it or saying it privately might help. Shortening the passage might also be helpful. If a child struggles to read aloud, make it optional in your session— call on volunteers.

4. Simplify instructions. Give one direction at a time. Back up your verbal instructions with written or picture cues.

5. Use multiple presentation tools. Involve as many of the senses as possible. Tell the story, have pictures of the characters, offer a short movie of the story, have figurines to move for a story re-telling, or use drama. If a child struggles in one area, there will be another presentation mode that will help a child process the information.

6. Use multiple response tools. Offer choices. Some children may want to write an answer, speak an answer, draw a picture, or make a PowerPoint slideshow to respond to the message.

7. Remember the main thing: Church is not school. Free the child from those difficult academic areas so that he or she is able to focus on developing a relationship with Jesus Christ.

Resources:

1. *The Complete Learning Disabilities Handbook: Ready-to-Use Strategies and Activities for Teaching Students with Learning Disabilities* by Joan M. Harwell and Rebecca Williams Jackson (Jossey-Bass, 2008)

2. *Learning Disabilities and the Church: Including All God's Kids in Your Education and Worship.* Cynthia Holder Rich and Martha Ross-Mockaitis (Faith Alive Christian Resources)

3. LD Online, http://www.ldonline.org

Speech and Language Impairments

Description:

For some children, speaking is difficult. Certain letter sounds or words might be difficult to produce. Some children might stutter, repeating certain sounds or words. Other children are easy to understand and the concern is in language concepts. That child might struggle to find the right word to express an idea or struggle to organize a sentence correctly. Other children might struggle to follow directions and comprehend spoken words. Some children may have very little ability to use spoken words and may even struggle with eating due to the differences in mouth structure or muscle weakness. All of these areas of difference fall under the category of speech and language impairments.

Characteristics:

May Occur with Other Impairments

Sometimes children have only speech and/or language impairments. Other times a child might have a speech and language issue because of another area of concern. A child with, for example, Down syndrome may struggle with speech and language issues. A child with cerebral palsy or a learning disability may also have difficulties with either speaking or language issues.

Speech

Speaking is actually a very complex system of muscle movements and coordination. It involves rhythm, airflow, voice quality, tone quality, volume, pitch, and the coordination of mouth and tongue muscles to quickly produce multiple variations in sounds. Infants are unable to speak words to communicate wants and needs, although the crying mechanism certainly communicates loudly and clearly. As a child grows, doctors and educators are listening for certain milestones in what a child is able to say and how they say it. When a child falls behind peers, sometimes a referral is made to a speech and language therapist in order to evaluate the differences.

Language

Language describes a child's ability to understand and use words effectively. Sometimes children struggle to use correct grammar or choose a correct word to fit the meaning of their idea. Children might have limited vocabulary or struggle to understand directions. A child may become frustrated when he knows what he wants to say but can't seem to communicate the thoughts accurately to others.

Language is only one form of communication; some children who struggle with language often find other ways to communicate. Sometimes a child might take your hand and pull you to an object. A child might start to throw a tantrum or cry in response to your request. A child might withdraw or act out when his words are not sufficient. Remember to put some of these behaviors in perspective. What would you do if you could not tell someone what you were thinking or what you might need or want?

Interventions:

1. Learn the child's language system by having casual conversations with him beyond your classroom time. Knowing a child's sound substitutions or how to use his communication device can help you engage in conversation more effectively. It's critical that you know how a child will communicate when she needs to use the bathroom or when she needs help. Know the basics.

2. Think of ways around the language concern whenever possible. Use visuals, figurines, pictures, PowerPoint slides, or picture/word schedules to communicate with the child.

3. Understand the difference between receptive language and expressive language. Some children may struggle to speak (expressive), but that same child may understand language (receptive) quite well. Learn about the child's exact areas of gifts and concerns.

4. Be patient. You typically don't need to speak more loudly. It might be helpful to slow down a bit when you speak, shorten

your sentences, and emphasize key words repeatedly. It also might help to ask a question and then wait . . . wait . . . wait. Give that child a chance to process and respond. Many times we are too quick to jump in with a cue or repeat the question while the child is still processing.

5. Listen for the meaning behind what is said. Sometimes you can see that a child is excited but you understand very few of the words that the child just spoke. "I see you are excited," lets the child know you understood. Don't just focus on the spoken words but on the body language, facial expression, and gestures.

6. When you don't understand a child's words, you could ask that child to repeat what was said, request that she say it a different way, or offer some choices of what you might have heard to see if a child will agree with your best guesses. Some children can sing an answer, write an answer, or point to an answer where spoken words might fail. Get to know the individual.

Resources:

1. American Speech-Language-Hearing Association (ASHA), http://www.asha.org
2. *Child Speech, Language and Listening Problems: What Every Parent Should Know* by Patricia McAleer Hamaguchi (Wiley, 2001)
3. *Inclusion for Children with Speech and Language Impairments: Accessing the Curriculum and Promoting Personal and Social Development* by Kate Ripley, Jenny Barrett, and Pam Fleming (David Fulton Publishers, 2001)
4. *The Inclusive Learning Center Book for Preschool Children with Special Needs* by Christy Isbell and Rebecca Isbell (Gryphon House, 2005)

Spina Bifida

Description:

Spina bifida indicates that an individual has an incomplete closure in the spinal column. In mild forms of spina bifida, there might be openings in the spinal column but no damage to the spinal cord. Some forms can be repaired with surgery, and there is no damage to the spinal cord. The more severe type, however, happens when a portion of the spinal cord itself protrudes through the back, many times exposing tissue and nerves. It is this more severe type we will discuss in this section.

Characteristics:

Muscle Weakness and Paralysis

Most children experience muscle weakness or paralysis downward from the open spot on the spine. It's common to see children use crutches, walkers, or wheelchairs. It's also common that children struggle with bowel and bladder control.

Hydrocephalus

It's very common for children with spina bifida to have a buildup of fluid, which can pool in the brain. This is called hydrocephalus. A shunt (drain) is surgically implanted to help drain the fluid. Without that drain, or if the shunt malfunctions, a child might suffer significant issues such as brain damage or seizures. It's important to know if a child has a shunt. If a child were to fall on his shunt, he may require medical attention.

Learning

Sometimes children with spina bifida can have a variety of issues related to learning. Some children have a difficult time paying attention or have speech and language concerns. Others may struggle in academic areas and need special support. Other children may have no additional issues aside from the physical differences associated with spina bifida.

Self-Care

Many children will require catheterization or diapering. It's important to find out about the self-care needs of the child you are serving. Older children may be able to do the catheterization on their own, but will need access to a private area for the purpose.

Interventions:

1. Become comfortable with the child's self-care needs. Make sure you have a written bathroom policy and written permission from parents to assist a child when needed. This should always be done with two adults, at least one of them trained by parents to complete the routine.

2. Make physical arrangements for the child. Is the child able to sit on the floor? Scoot? Move from chair to floor without help? Will the child need space to safely maneuver in a wheelchair or walker? Can the child access all parts of the building where you will be meeting? The best way to find out is to interview the parents and student, determine

their equipment needs, and then borrow the same piece of equipment. Sit in that wheelchair and try to move around your facility. Use a walker and try to move around the table or seats in your area. Many times this will give you insight into what needs to be altered to best support this child.

3. Understand any safety concerns with the child's medical condition, especially their shunt. Make sure each leader is aware of any emergency procedures and provide printed details for all.

4. Know the child's individual gifts and needs. You may need to access other tips and ideas from various sections in this guide based on the additional concerns. If, for example, a child struggles in the speech and language area, reference that section for more ideas on how to set up a successful experience at church.

5. Make sure peers are comfortable with some of the mobility equipment. Letting them ask questions about braces, standers, walkers, and wheelchairs can allow children to be more comfortable. Borrowing a second set of equipment will allow peers to try it out and see what it might be like to use a walker or wheelchair.

Resources:

1. *Children with Spina Bifida: A Parents' Guide* edited by Marlene Lutkenhoff (Woodbine House, 2007)

2. *Helping Kids Include Kids with Disabilities* by Barbara J. Newman (Faith Alive Christian Resources, 2001)

3. Spina Bifida Association of America, http://www.spinabifidaassociation.org

Tourette Syndrome

Description:

Tourette syndrome is a neurological (brain) difference that shows up in the body in the form of tics as well as unwanted vocalizations. Tourette syndrome is often first noticed in the elementary ages. While some people have a picture of children yelling out obscenities or making inappropriate remarks, this is actually true in only a small number of children. Boys are more frequently diagnosed with Tourette syndrome than girls.

Characteristics:

Tics

Tics are involuntary, rapid, and sudden movements. Children with tics might shrug their shoulders, blink their eyes quickly, make certain facial movements, or have more involved tics such as hopping or bending.

Vocalizations

Repeated vocal outbursts can also be common. These might be simple vocalizations like clearing of the throat, grunting, or sniffing. It might also involve words or phrases. For a small number of individuals, those words and phrases might be obscenities.

Brain Difference, Not A Behavior Difference

Many times it's easy to think that someone should just "stop" or "get it under control" or "be more mature." Tourette syndrome, however, is not a behavioral choice. It would be similar to telling a child having seizures to "stop" or "be more mature." That simply does not make sense.

Treatment

For most people, no treatment is necessary. In fact, the tics or vocalizations may be so minor that the individual is not aware he or she has Tourette syndrome. For those who would like to control the tics, however, as they are troubling for that person, medications are available.

Interventions:

1. It's important as a group leader to understand clearly what to expect from the child with Tourette syndrome. Understand what movements or words might be involved, and also understand how the child may want you to support him or her.

2. Discuss with parents and the child what might be important for the peers to know. If the body movements or words will be noticeable to the other children, consider giving them information to best receive the individual as part of the group. Some children might want to explain it to peers themselves.

3. While some children have combinations of learning differences, Tourette syndrome is not associated with any other learning or physical differences. A child with Tourette syndrome is not, for example, more likely to struggle with

reading or attention. It is true, however, that some children have more than one area of difference. That could be true with any child.

Resources:
1. *Kids in the Syndrome Mix of ADHD, LD, Asperger's, Tourette's, Bipolar and More!: The One Stop Guide for Parents, Teachers, and Other Professionals* by Martin L. Kutscher, Robert R. Wolff, and Tony Attwood (Jessica Kingsley Publishers, 2007)
2. National Tourette Syndrome Association, http://tsa-usa.org

Traumatic Brain Injury (TBI)

Description:
A traumatic brain injury happens when there is an injury to the brain after a person is hit in the head or is shaken violently. The injury can impact how a child acts, thinks, and moves. This term is not used for a child who is born with a brain injury or damage that happens during the birthing process. Because the brain is responsible for many different functions, the result usually corresponds with the area or areas that were damaged. For example, head injuries might cause changes in how a child thinks or reasons, uses and understands words, remembers, pays attention, problem solves, behaves, moves, sees, or hears.

Characteristics:
Mild to Severe
TBI can range from mild to severe, depending on the type and extent of the injury.

Change Over Time
The impact of the injury can change over time. With help and therapy, the brain may compensate for the injury and the child will experience great improvement. It's also possible that additional areas of concern may creep in as the child grows and more is expected from her.

Possible Physical Changes
TBI can impact any one of the sensory systems. A child may struggle with areas such as sight, hearing, speaking, moving, and balance. Some children may have seizures or headaches.

Possible Changes in Thinking

A child may struggle with areas of memory or attention. Learning academic skills might become more difficult for the child. Talking and listening might be an area of struggle. Basically, the changes in thinking will be caused by the area impacted by the injury.

Possible Social or Emotional Changes

Because areas of the brain are also responsible for mood regulation, emotions, social skills, impulse control, and other aspects of personality, any one of these areas can experience change and may result in behavior problems.

Interventions:

1. Get to know the child. Find out about the injury and what areas of gifts and needs the child currently has.

2. It's possible that your church community walked with the family through the time of injury. You may have known the child prior to the event. You will need to prepare yourself to get reacquainted with the child. Sometimes the changes in personality can be the most dramatic for those who have known the child over time.

3. Have a consistent routine and a predictable environment. This will help a child adjust to your setting and know what to expect each week. Give advance warning for changes in your schedule.

4. While being consistent and predictable, it's also important to be flexible. A child may tire easily, need frequent breaks, or take extra time to answer a question or finish an activity.

5. Use multiple sensory tools in your worship and education. Sounds, sights, smells, tastes, and items to touch will all support new learning as well as connect with past learning.

6. Be patient. If an area such as short-term memory is affected, that skill may never fully return. You may need to repeat the directions multiple times, direct a child to a written list, or find alternate ways around that area of concern. When that child asks you the same question each day (or multiple times a day), she truly does not know the answer.

7. Remember that his peers may also need to become reacquainted with this friend. Be sensitive to their questions and comments.

8. Focus on the strength areas. While it's easy to think about what has been altered or lost, there will be many strong areas. Make sure to highlight those skills as part of your group.

Resources:

1. *Children with Traumatic Brain Injury: A Parents' Guide* (The Special Needs Collection) edited by Lisa Schoenbrodt (Woodbine House, 2001)

2. National Resource Center for Traumatic Brain Injury, http://www.neuro.pmr.vcu.edu

3. TBI Resource Guide, http://www.neuroskills.com/children.shtml

Visual Impairments

Description:

There are many possible causes of visual impairments. A child might have eye infections, cataracts, congenital issues, or one of many other eye disorders that cause difficulties in being able to see. A child might be known as partially sighted, low vision, legally blind, or totally blind. Some of those children have visual impairment from birth, and others acquire a visual impairment at a later age.

Characteristics:

Partially Sighted

This term refers to a child who has some kind of vision problem and requires support of some kind to use the vision they have.

Low Vision

Even with glasses or contact lenses, this child will have difficulty reading something like a newspaper or book at a distance that most people could see without difficulty.

Legally Blind

This term is used when a child has less than 20/200 vision in her better eye. This means she needs to be as close as twenty feet to see what another person can see at two hundred feet.

Totally Blind
A child who is totally blind may have learned to read using Braille or in some other non-visual way.

Age of Onset
Some children have a certain amount of sight when they are younger, and they have had a chance to experience and explore the world with their vision. Others have not had that chance and do not have a visual concept for something like "purple" or "cloud."

Interactions
Some children with visual impairments struggle with social interactions, as they find it difficult to read body language or pick up on visual cues.

Interventions:

1. Know what supports are helpful for the child and have them available at church. If a child uses larger print, then find or make your materials with larger print. If a child reads using Braille, be prepared with reading materials using that format. If special lighting or pieces of technology can help a child, have that available.

2. Be cautious with PowerPoint presentations. Remember that your child will only be able to hear the material, not see it. Make sure to communicate the information covered in the PowerPoint slides in some other form as well.

3. Keep your physical environment consistent and free from clutter. Unexpectedly moving chairs or other objects can make it hazardous for a child who is expecting the room to be in the same arrangement as the last time. Give warning when you move furniture or supplies.

4. Provide information through multiple sensory channels. While other children will benefit from the visuals you bring to your worship and education settings, a child with a visual impairment will appreciate auditory, tactile, and other sensory input.

5. Know how to best support movement in a safe way. Under what circumstance should you assist the child and how should you assist?

6. Facilitate social interactions. Some children will need assistance to know when and how to enter into play or other informal activities with friends.

Resources:

1. *Children with Visual Impairments: A Guide for Parents* by M. Cay Holbrook (Woodbine House, 2006)

2. *Helping Children Who Are Blind* (Early Assistance Series for Children with Disabilities) by Sandy Niemann and Namita Jacob (Hesperian Foundation, 2000)

3. *Look At It This Way: Toys and Activities with Children Who Have Visual Impairments* by Roma Lear (Butterworth-Heinemann, 1998)

4. National Federation of the Blind, http://www.nfb.org

5

Support: The Staff Who Know the Kids

One of the keys to growth and flourishing of ministry to and with children with learning differences is support of the staff and volunteers. These people are often the front line for interaction with the kids and their families. For this reason, proper hiring, training, and support for both paid and volunteer staff are fundamental—even if the form that takes varies widely based on the size and resources of a church. The goal is to work with your staff to create an atmosphere of response rather than reaction that first and foremost seeks to help kids leave each Sunday feeling affirmed.

Hiring and Supervision

In the interview and hiring process or in the process of engaging volunteers, list work with learning differences as part of the job outline. Ask about the applicant's background, comfort, and expertise with learning differences; some people may have formal education that involves learning differences in one way or another. Many may have had more "informal" experience than they realize. Talk with them about their life experiences, whether professional or not. Do their own children have learning differences, or perhaps have had the question raised at some point? Have they worked with friends and family on these issues? In their professional lives, have they come across situations that required ability to understand different ways of teaching and learning? What is the profile of their personal learning style? Help them name and affirm the insights and experience they may already have had.

Above all, reassure staff that they don't have to have special training to begin a real relationship with the kids and parents. To be intentional and authentic is the best beginning. Their honesty with parents about wanting to help and needing to learn how will form the best relationship on which to build.

- Be sure staff know all the basic welcoming procedures and the reasons for them, including having parents fill out forms, being proactive with newer parents about including and understanding all children, and inviting any special information about their child.

- As discussed in the section on Curricula in Chapter 3, make it clear that adapting lesson plans for particular groups and individuals does take intentional planning. By incorporating that into the working awareness and job descriptions for staff, we can help teachers to see it as a natural—and not an exceptional— expectation, but also one that is supported and acknowledged by supervisors and clergy. Thus the advance work becomes a normal part of the job, whether paid or volunteer, rather than being invisible work that can cause resentment on the part of the worker.

- Remind staff about the importance of language and how we refer to people with difference or disability. Review with them the use of person-centered language and talking to parents about their preferences. Remind them also that the language they use will be the language other children and teens learn to use, as well.

- Have staff be careful using wording such as "God doesn't give us more than we can bear," or "You must have done something special to get such a special child," with parents. (See the Theology section in Chapter 8.) As one mom of a child with Down syndrome said, "My child isn't a spiritual prop, meant to teach us or reward us." Staff should be with parents in whatever *they* are feeling, but there's no need for staff to judge or explain it back to them, which is usually simply a sign of the staff person's own anxiety and better brought to a supervisor than to the family themselves.

- Be sure staff understand confidentiality issues—especially important with lay volunteers who understandably may find themselves at a church event being asked questions by another parent about a child they observed ("What's the deal with that kid?"). At that moment, the staff person needs to understand that they themselves wear the hat not of a congregant, but of a pastoral caregiver to the child and his family, which calls for confidentiality. Help them to have answers ready such as, "I'll let that be their story to tell," or "I'm in conversation with her parents about her particular needs," or simply "I need to let that remain confidential for now." That, in turn, helps the individuals understand that their own family would be treated with the same confidentiality.

- If a child needs one-on-one assistance in the classroom from an adult rather than a peer buddy, help teachers find the right person or team of people for the child; try not to put that burden on the family unless they already have someone they prefer to use. Reach into the church community, using the congregational guides or a network system. Perhaps someone who doesn't have a young child at that point in time, someone with training or experience, or maybe even a teen, can be with that child for an hour in Sunday School. That person needs to be appropriately matched, trained, and also aware of confidentiality issues.

Beyond the church, staff or clergy can offer to go to school team interviews or IEP (Individualized Educational Plan) meetings with parents—not to intervene but to simply be present and show support. Be sure the individuals who take on this level of professional responsibility are trained and aware of what they should and shouldn't do in that particular role, as well as of confidentiality in all situations throughout the congregation.

Training

Training (in whatever form it's possible and available, and even if it feels like a small step) helps empower staff. It alleviates their own anxiety, gives them specific tools, and addresses particular behavioral challenges and learning differences among children. Help make information available to your staff about local training by non-church sources. Check with local professionals for recommendations.

Partner with other churches to bring in a special education consultant for a workshop. Be sure the consultant respects different faith traditions and understands the needs she would be addressing. Will the staff need time to tell their individual stories and questions? Do they need a "takeaway," such as lists of tips and resources for specific challenges? Work with the presenter in advance to make sure she can meet the group where they are.

Training sessions within the congregation are important, even if they function mainly as staff and clergy support and visioning. If there is a special needs consultant available from your diocese, judicatory, or community, invite him in for the appropriate parts of the discussion. You can also tap people in your congregations who have related professional backgrounds, such as a special education teacher, an occupational therapist, or a high school teacher whose class includes a range of learning styles. That person can join the discussion in a way that lets them bring their experience to bear on the immediate questions and situations at hand.

Whether you have access to a consultant or trained church member, spend a morning talking about questions and issues, offering suggestions that staff and clergy have from their own resources, reminding everyone that learning and mistakes are part of the process, and, above all, reinforcing the mission to serve all children as best we can:

- Talk about the theology of difference and disability, in a way appropriate to the group.
- Share examples of children and families who have been supported by the congregation.
- Talk about those families who may not yet feel supported or included.
- Allow for staff to share feelings, including fear and frustration, while making it clear that by sharing them among staff, families don't end up having to bear the brunt of those feelings.
- Ask in advance for questions on specific learning needs and strategies; prepare answers, materials, or further referrals as best you can.
- Share lesson plans, activities, and formats that have been used, and what has been more and less effective with them.
- If you have past volunteers, "buddies," or faith partners, invite them to meet with newer volunteers in the context of this training.
- Brainstorm about next steps in how events, including worship, may better include specific children and families.
- Remind everyone of the basic outlines of pastoral confidentiality and who each person's contact is for pastoral issues that arise.

Abuse Prevention Programs

Finally, follow your church's policy for abuse prevention training. In the Episcopal Church, for example, all staff who work with children and teens must complete the "Safe Church" program once every five years. Learn what your denomination's policies are. Keep copies of your staff's training certificates in their personnel files.

Resources

Church resources:

1. As much as possible within your budget, support staff with printed and video materials and resources (see the Bibliography on page 95). Invite them to join e-mail lists of local or regional networks that support and serve people with disabilities in faith communities.

2. Develop relationships with local psychologists or school counselors who specialize in learning differences and family support. When possible, have them available for staff to consult with on specific issues, as agreed upon by the staff supervisor and clergy.

3. Once parents have opened up deeper discussion with staff about their child's difference, consider the appropriateness of suggesting to them that one key staff person develop a direct connection with the child's teacher at school or another support person (counselor or psychologist) to learn more about working with the child. Though potentially very helpful, this option must be approached carefully and only with staff, lay or volunteer, who understand boundary and confidentiality issues and for a child whose differences seem appropriate to this step.

Regional denominational resources:

Denominational support varies widely, but make sure to be in touch with the local and regional staff—particularly those who lead Christian Formation and youth programs—about what's available. Encourage and support them in their development of networks and resources for churches in your judicatory.

Possibilities include: online resources through the adjudicatory website; video and printed materials through its library; a network of Christian educators, both lay and ordained; a network or task force of people with a particular focus or interest in integrating special-needs children and teens; and specialists, such as family counselors or special education teachers, who have either a formal or a referral type of relationship with the denomination. Your church may need to take the lead in creating area partnership around these issues.

Emotional Support

Throughout all your work with staff, make it clear that they are always welcome to come talk to you—as lay supervisor or clergy—in a personal way about a frustration or a success. This will help develop relationships among staff and clergy that supersede job descriptions, allowing them to feel they are known and supported as people.

Allow for all of someone's feelings and questions, including those that don't seem correct and that they may feel hesitant to express. Let them share frustrations and fears. What's important is that it's shared in relationship to you, and not the parents or the child. Often the chance to express and process feelings is, in itself, what allows a staff person to move beyond them in a transformative and hopeful way.

Be sure the supervisor and staff have regular and comfortable ways to be in touch, whether informal meetings, structured meetings, or by phone. Allow them to feel free to talk on a regular basis without feeling like it takes an exceptional effort. At the same time, be aware that using technology to communicate about more sensitive and confidential feelings and pastoral matters may be inappropriate. You may want to confine your most honest discussions to those that are spoken, not written.

As always, give acknowledgement and recognition to your teachers, both in liturgy and in more individual settings. If there's a staff person or volunteer who has done especially intensive, effective work with a child or teen, be sure to acknowledge and thank them, making sure supervisors and clergy are aware of it.

Reaching Out

Clergy and staff need to take on the role of being the askers—"How can we help? How can we better understand?"—instead of leaving that role to the parents, which usually falls to them in other situations. Like Jesus calling out to the woman who was bent over and unable to stand straight (Luke 13:10–17), the church needs to be the one taking on the role of reaching out to someone who may be hesitant to name their struggles.

Remember that a key part of success in establishing and growing in relationship with families is the stability of the staff they encounter. The more support and recognition the staff receive, the better the church will be at retaining trained, experienced people well known and familiar to the children and parents.

6

Pray: The Community in Worship

Worship lies at the heart of what defines faith communities as being about faith—or the hope for it. Integrated, intergenerational worship is perhaps the most important space to experiencing belonging and integration, full of rich and sensual possibilities. Indeed, those are the possibilities we commit to when we, as a congregation, surround a child being baptized and promise to do everything in our power to support that person's life in Christ. Yet some of the most challenging questions around worship that integrates children and teens with learning differences are the most basic:

Welcoming

- Are ushers and greeters truly prepared to say—and mean— "Welcome," and, if they see a new family with a child, ask if there is anything they can do to help that family feel comfortable in the service? Do ushers and greeters seem jarred or annoyed or act like it's a problem if someone asks for assistance for herself or for a child? Is it treated as out of the norm? Or is it incorporated like any other "normal" need or request such as where the bathroom is?

- If you don't have a requested type of assistance, are ushers and greeters trained to say, "I'm so sorry we don't have that in place yet. Can we talk after the service about what would be most helpful and the best way to go about doing it?" The transition to this way of responding to particular needs may take time and training in which the welcoming team can express and address their own discomforts and questions.

- As ushers and greeters become more comfortable with asking questions and figuring out answers, they can even be enabled to do it with a sense of humor and ease that communicates to everyone the joy we can all feel in supporting each other's humanness.

Comfort with Noise and Silence

Welcoming and encouraging children of all ages in worship is impacted by lots of factors, including the tradition and culture of your congregation, whether its liturgical practices are considered high or low, whether you've had a family-friendly service in the past or present, and whether you've had a service specifically intended for children. But wherever you are on the spectrum, it's important to begin right there, working inclusion into the place you already are without losing things you don't want to lose.

Worship is always an area vulnerable to fear of loss, usually articulated as "We've always done it that way," or "This is our tradition." Know in advance that some people will be uncomfortable with a shift in worship practices, especially if your congregation has not been raising awareness of constructively and intentionally incorporating children into worship. Be prepared to listen to their concerns without absorbing their fears or anxiety. Their needs and concerns are as much "on the table" as those of families with children. Everyone can bend a little bit, and indeed equilibrium usually finds itself more easily than people expect.

Include open discussion of the topic of integrating children into worship—whatever your particular approach will be—in education forums on worship, with the worship team or committee, with strategic planning, and in welcome literature. Acknowledge that children need to be children, and that supports such as clipboards and books need to be provided, while at the same time acknowledging that children can learn reverence (which is not the same thing as severity, stiffness, or being completely quiet) from the adults around them. As they see their parents, teachers, and other adults model reverence, interest, and attention, they will too. For some children, having their "buddy" or faith partner with them in worship may be helpful.

Be aware of our wonderful traditions of multi-sensory worship. These days, the term is often associated with emergent church or non-traditional settings. But in fact, "multi-sensory worship" is as old as the hills, from stained glass to incense to intentional movement within a holy space. Most people in churches up until the Renaissance and Enlightenment could not read, so litany, statues, stories in stained glass and paintings, icons, incense, and music were all part of the worship experience. Worship is sensual, and paying attention to that in the context of your particular culture will affect how kids—and adults who also have different ways of responding to the sensual world around them—engage it.

A final observation I've made is that those who might seem most reactive to the idea of children's noise in worship (usually before they've actually experienced much of it) are often the same people who are uncomfortable with real and intentional silence in worship, as well. For these members of your community, it may take time and community dialogue around the topic of worship for them to begin to realize the issue isn't really about either sound or silence but about fear or anxiety that arises in them in either case. The sooner they feel safe in expressing those feelings, the more fully they will feel connected to the renewed worship going on around them.

Helping Younger Children

Have folders or clipboards (the kind that open up to hold pencils and crayons are especially effective) for kids during the service. Each week the clipboard can hold age-appropriate activity sheets related to the Revised Common Lectionary reading for the day, such as those downloaded free at http://www.homiliesbyemail.com/leaf/activity-sheets.html, or something else appropriate to your denomination's services. You can use color-coded dots to show which, for instance, are for ages four to six, and which are for ages seven to ten. Be sure your greeters know to be proactive in directing families to these resources.

Have a basket or shelf of soft toys and picture books in the entry area of the church. This will not only serve the practical purpose of providing entertainment for young children, it also demonstrates a welcoming attitude toward visiting families.

You can use the guides or faith partners to help here, too—to support parents and kids. Parents often feel better knowing what to expect and what guidelines to give their kids (when to be quiet, when to move, etc.). People often want to honor the structure that's in place and are more comfortable when they feel they can find their own place within that. So offer a description of your process of worship, such as when there are different kinds of silence, speech, music, and movement—but emphasize that it's adaptable and flexible.

It can be helpful to invite kids and their parents, especially if they are new, to come into the church with the clergy or teacher apart from worship. Let the child explore, help her see and touch, with reverence, the altar area and other symbols of your faith, and give age-appropriate responses about what your members do and don't do, and when and why. This interaction will vary greatly, based on the child's age and learning difference. For example, a young child with ADHD may be most aided by being allowed to run around the space and in and out of all places she can't usually go during worship; conversely, a child with autism may appreciate the reinforcement that a certain space is a quiet or still space. Whatever ends up making it feel comfortable and familiar for the child can be hugely helpful in making him and his family feel at home in the worship space.

Leading Worship

If it's part of your tradition to use children and teens as acolytes, include those children with learning differences in ways that you and their parents see as appropriate. Such inclusion in leading worship actually empowers them even more to embody and engage the rhythms of worship; children who might have trouble connecting with the worship can become very attentive and engaged when helping lead it. Children respond to the responsibility. Parents may sit with them, if needed—for instance, in an acolyte pew, if that works in your space. Especially with younger children, involving them in any role takes adult attention and maintenance, but it also serves as a lovely and clear message of welcome and inclusion. Many adults, especially seniors, love seeing the joyous and enthusiastic responses of children as they participate in worship.

Remind people, especially your worship leadership, that having families feel comfortable integrating their children into worship is actually a wonderful opportunity to look at the whole notion of reverence as something that shows how we truly revere God, rather than as stiffness or severity. As adults mine the richness of how they revere God together—reflecting on their own focus and participation in the worship, while being sensitive to the holiness of space and sound, movement and ritual—they will model for and lead children and teens into reverence. Additionally, children often have a keen sense of the holy and can model for the community a sense of reverence and awe that adults may have forgotten in their adherence to protocol.

Approach integrating those with various ways of learning into worship as an opportunity to expand your liturgical resources. This can open up more deeply the potential of your particular tradition without leaving its basic structures and gifts behind.

Look at your weekly worship schedule to see if there is a service that more readily lends itself to leadership by kids with learning differences. Again, this is not toward creating a separate service for them, but finding ways for the entire community to experience their presence and leadership. For example, many faith communities have a Sunday evening or midweek service. In addition to incorporating children and teens into your community's primary service (such as Sunday morning), see if one of the other weekly services has the flexibility and atmosphere to, for instance, have children come forward to assist in ritual, engage in the homily (whether in questions and answers, storytelling, or a skit), dance, or create the music. Again, a smaller, more intimate service might more readily lend itself to this experimentation, for both children or adults.

Feeling They Belong

For families with a child or teen with a hearing impairment, ask them what would be most helpful, even if it may take time and planning to put those assists in place. Does the child need sign language? Or a hearing-aid system where she sits? Would printed versions of the liturgy be most helpful? Again, even if you don't have those things onhand immediately, your question assures the family that you are working with them to figure it out.

Where kids sit matters: For many children and teens, they'll pay more attention if they're closer to the action. Have ushers and other congregants invite families toward the front, though the families may choose otherwise. If a kid is very sensitive to sound, or certain visuals, help her find the best place to sit—not to imply keeping them out of the way but to make clear you're really trying to find the place that she is most comfortable. For instance, if she's sensitive to sound, it may be upsetting to be too close to a musical instrument, while, conversely, a child who responds well to music may like being as close to the musicians as he can be as long as it doesn't distract the musicians (and many musicians may enjoy the subtle interaction with a nearby child).

The music program itself—whether through a choir, or simply through participating in congregational song—can be a wonderful way for some children to connect to the range of ways of being in worship, including the difference between a reflective, meditative moment (as with a repeated chant) or a joyous Gloria or hymn. There is much excellent yet simpler music available now, such as chants, rounds, or "paperless" music. Much of it in no way sacrifices excellence for being accessible, and it's appropriate for people of all ages. Teachers can incorporate it into Sunday School lessons, kids can use it in their regular moments of movement, gathering, or transition in Sunday School, and then they recognize it and can more vigorously participate when it is part of the community's worship.

Have children and teens be an active and visible part of the music ministry, in a way appropriate to the role of music in your community's programs and worship. Your musical leaders will need the same support and dialogue as other staff in meeting and understanding kids with learning differences where they are. Music frequently becomes a highly successful venue for experiencing community, affirmation, and faith, when other means, such as verbal and visual, are not as successful for a child.

Liturgy

In regards to coming forward for Holy Communion, ask the parents of a child with learning differences if it's easier for them to come forward first or at some other point in the process. If you have ushers who guide the congregation, be sure they're in direct conversation with the family about when they'd like to come forward, so that it feels smooth and unobtrusive to the family during the service itself.

For rituals such as baptism and communion, as with other aspects of community life, let yourself and those leading worship be open to how a child or teen engages the mystery of the sacrament. Baptism and communion are wonderful questions we live and relive into our entire lives, the mystery and meaning of which even those with extensive experience and intelligence cannot fully grasp. Often children and teens engage that mystery with a freshness that does not depend on waiting until they can "understand" the sacrament—which, of course, is a moment none of us can reach.

Within your worship tradition, be sure to make full use of the psalms. The psalms of joy are often ways for children with differences to join into poetic and musical expressions of their own words of joy. On the other hand, a psalm of lament might be just what a frustrated or frightened parent needed on that day. The range of psalms affirms the range of our dialogue with God, which families of children with learning differences may often assume they must self-edit.

Balance of Needs

Worship is one of the areas in which a congregation's fears arise before the reality has a chance to play out. Intentionally create an atmosphere of patience and nonjudgmentalism in worship, one based on understanding that including people and especially children with differences is all a work in process and that there's nothing to fear. As with any change in worship, people may fear the loss of something they need. Some will respond better to the effort to broaden how that looks, some will be more resistant, but trust that a middle ground will emerge. Help people to be open to the possibilities of being awed by "different" expressions of faith.

People are more reasonable when they are not surprised. Make it part of the larger formation and education of the community; again, include it in articles in the newsletter and topics in adult forum, and use illustrations about children's expressions of faith in sermons. Come in the side door, so to speak. Don't present it as "You have to let kids be noisy," but as theological, "How do we show God's inclusive and expansive love and how are we experiencing it ourselves?"

7

Lead: The Clergy

If welcoming children with learning differences and their families is to be a transformational part of a congregation's culture, the clergy need to seek, support, and embody it on a human and theological basis, not just as another political-correctness task. Since clergy carry much responsibility for naming the theology of our actions (What does this say we believe about God?) and enabling the actions that come from our theology (What does our idea of God mean for how we are with each other?), their theological understanding and pastoral support of the issues of learning differences in children are crucial to the church's efforts.

General

Clergy need to be intentionally aware of a broad and basic theological question: How do those with differences or disabilities affect us? Even if they've had sound theological training, it's important for clergy to get to know the way the questions work in contemporary language and specifically around the topics of difference/disability. Clergy need to be aware of the two edges to the question: (1) that those with disabilities evoke our fears of places in ourselves; and (2) that the "us" is illusory, since we are all disabled in different ways. Ultimately, clergy are most effective when they understand and believe that confronting that two-sided question gives everyone in the congregation the chance to be more inclusive of others and of the parts they fear within themselves—which is healing for the whole community.

Even for those clergy familiar with the theology of disability, there's always more to explore. The question of children's learning differences is usually a smaller piece of the larger desire to integrate those with disabilities. Steps clergy can take include reading more recent theological studies (see the Bibliography for a suggested list); being part of a local or regional network of clergy who support the full integration of those with disabilities; getting more familiar with the specific kids and situations their staff are encountering in classes and community events; exploring liturgical and prayer resources with families affected by learning differences; and—mainly—asking questions, then listening, listening, listening.

Clergy need to intentionally lead the faith community through the "preposition sequence" for those with difference/disability—from ministry *to* them, to ministry *for* them, to ministry *with* them, and finally to discovering the ministry *of* those with differences and disability. To understand that sequence, and how most churches are still stuck at "to" or "for," is to live into deeper relationship with others simply as fellow ministers of God's love, each of us according to our different ways.

Arriving at ministry *by* those with differences is the truly transformative stage, turning around our ideas of care giving and care receiving. How does it transform us when we receive care from people with clear differences or disabilities? Could it even take the form of a child who is patient with our frustrations and limitations? Could that be one form of ministry by someone with a disability? Or to be helped in some way by someone we would see ourselves as helping—does it remind us of our human frailty, perhaps the frailties we fear the most within ourselves? Does that person, in effect, help us to confront our fears and thus to be freer of them? The "preposition progression" breaks down our internal barriers and the fears within us.

Work to create an environment in which the clergy and staff are the "askers" instead of automatically leaving that role to the family. Parents, especially those with kids with differences, so often end up being the ones who do the work of asking all the questions in any new situation. Work with staff to avoid pinning the questions of difference and fear on the child or family with the learning difference. The fears and the heightened awareness of differences are about us all.

Ultimately, the theological and managerial guidance of clergy is indispensible to the congregation's ability to ask the question, "Do we really believe you belong here, or are we just saying it" and to answer, "Yes, we really believe it."

Pastoral Care

In offering pastoral care to families of children with learning differences, clergy should be careful to avoid the traps of wording like "'God doesn't give us more than we can bear," or "Everything is for a reason." Such phrases are usually ways of dealing with our own anxiety, but the point is to be with someone in their feelings, not to use them to correct our anxiety. Language that suggests things like personal tests or predestined events can only heighten a parent's fear and guilt, and do not project a compassionate and involved God.

Be careful with language that suggests reward/rebuke or blessing/curse, such as "God truly blessed you with such a special child." The implication can be that God didn't bless others; or the parent, who may be harassed and discouraged, may feel resentment at the idea of a God who would "bless" them in this way. If a parent uses such language, which people often do as a way of holding things together, offer an alternative without criticizing theirs. Most importantly, ask people to share their stories with you. Listen to the pain and hopes that arise.

Know that it's okay to answer simply "I don't know" to a question about how or why something like a difference or disability happened. Understand that for many families, healing comes through the faith community rather than through any one particular experience or explanation. Your authenticity will help them build trust in sharing their real feelings and experiences with the community, rather than an instinctual fear of the "right and wrong" feelings and answers that they fear they are supposed to deliver in order to be approved of by clergy.

Think creatively about pastoral support and even pastoral liturgy around life events that families with difference or disability are confronted with, such as during psychological or educational assessments or diagnosis. Allow parents to grieve the loss of what they had expected or hoped for in a child, while welcoming and blessing the gifts they didn't expect.

Notice and encourage the network within the faith community itself that may begin to arise on its own around the child or family. Help guide people with gifts of pastoral support or professional background toward the family, and structure support for the network and staff (see Chapter 2 on Church Atmosphere).

Help Create Language Around the Topic

If questions such as "How will such a person get anything out of the sermon?" or "How can they understand the liturgy/sacrament?" occur, turn the question around. How much does anyone get out of the sermon, how well does anyone understand the sacrament? As clergy, we can show that the questions apply to all of us.

As John H. Westerhoff notes in his paradigm for faith development, its stages are not like successive points on a timeline but rather like tree rings. At the core is experienced faith, then affiliative faith, searching faith, and owned faith (*Will Our Children Have Faith*, Morehouse Publishing, 2000, pp. 88–89). These phases *usually* correspond to life stages such as early and later childhood, adolescence, and adulthood. But all stages are equally valid, and indeed we rely on all stages throughout our lives, underlining that the most basic, experienced faith—which we usually do either in family, faith community, or both—is experiential. Thus correct "understanding" of theology or sacrament is not actually the goal of faith or the way in which we should most centrally recognize and celebrate faith. A congregation that doesn't wait for people to "understand" intellectual theological ideas in order to engage them in the mystery of God and God's people allows them all to see everyone, including those who may rely on experienced faith, as equal partners in the faith journey.

Language around difference and disability—both about how they are universal, and about how they can be specific and unique—can be lifted as a regular theological and scriptural strand out of sermons, Bible studies, adult forums, and church publications. Sometimes it may be appropriate to treat the topic separately, but it can also be woven in as part of inclusivity awareness in a way that need not take away from the other focuses of the congregation. Those who resist by saying, "We can't take away from our real focus to spend time on this secondary issue of kids with learning differences," can be answered by pointing out that inclusivity is part of our basic understanding of who God is and how God wants us to be. It's not a "separate agenda item." If clergy weave this theological foundation in intentionally and faithfully, then it's easier for people, over time, to absorb it.

Be mindful of interpretation of scriptural passages that suggest that disability is associated with sin or insufficient faith. Imagine how those with learning differences in their families might hear this. For instance, to say that we must all "look at our personal relationship with Jesus" may cause anxiety and fear in a parent whose child with autism is showing very different ways of relating that even she, as the child's mother, may feel left out of. Always circle back to the Gospel as embodied in the actions of Jesus Christ and his compassionate response to human beings who stood before him in need.

Finally, clergy should be careful to, in ways that are appropriate without being confessional, acknowledge that they have their own disabilities and limitations. We shouldn't be platitudinal; some people's logistical challenges are simply greater than those of others, and we need to respect each other's journeys. But neither should clergy embody the Pharisee's prayer— thanking God he wasn't like the other man.

Beyond the Congregation

Find out about your judicatory's resources, both the point person, if one exists, for support of difference/disability, and resources available through a library or online. Support and attend denominational and interfaith workshops and listen to what others are encountering, planning, and learning. Share your own congregation's experience.

Incorporate the question of difference and disability into regular clergy meetings, workshops, and conferences. Make sure that any ministry fair, for example, offers a session on some aspect—physical, programmatic, etc.—of those with differences or disabilities.

Connect with faith leaders from local congregations. Often a neighboring congregation of the same or a different faith may have been especially progressive in addressing the needs of those with differences and disabilities, particularly if a school is connected with the congregation. Meet with leaders; join local networks and email lists. Learn from others.

8

Believe: The Theology of Difference and Disability

Ministering to and with those who seem different from us, including those whose learning and intelligence styles differ from what we see as the norm, gives clergy, staff, and congregations the challenge and opportunity to look more closely at their own assumptions, comfort zones, and *dis*comfort zones. A faith community's dialogue around the theology of difference and disability is a chance to look more deeply at their "radical welcome," their belief in the breadth of God's love, and the reality of how that looks in their church day to day.[1]

As incorrect as it might seem, the only place anyone can begin to understand the theology of difference and disability is by examining what those terms evoke in them on the most basic level. Without that kind of baseline honesty, it becomes much more difficult to open ourselves up to true transformation. Does the idea of disability evoke fear, anger, confusion—compassion, groundedness, peace—or some combination of all of those? If we haven't reflected much on our shared, universal fears of being un-able,

---

[1] For much of the inspiration and resources in this section, I am indebted to Bill Gaventa, Associate Professor, the Elizabeth M. Boggs Center on Developmental Disabilities, New Brunswick, New Jersey, and his course *Ministry with Persons with Disabilities and Their Families*, Princeton Theological Seminary, January 2009.

of losing power and autonomy, then fear and denial can be understandable first responses. Or, alternatively, our experiences with our own minds and bodies, our families, and our life histories, including professional work, may already have brought us along a deepening journey of understanding of our own limitations, as well as familiarity with working with the limitations of others.

Difference and disability, however broadly or specifically you identify those things, hit squarely at the center of theology in that they bring up three of the most central questions of theology:

1. What does it mean to be a person?
2. What does it mean to be God?
3. Who are God's people?

Seminaries, conferences, and publications often place these questions into the category of either theology or pastoral care. But in fact, as with all theology and pastoral care, these questions are two sides of the same coin; in other words, the term "pastoral theology" is redundant. All three questions force us to examine how what we're saying about God affects what we say, and do, with community.

When we look at the more distant history of theological thinking, though disability as we think of it is rarely directly addressed, the classical theologians do imply things about disability. This thinking can be found in doctrines of creation, resurrection, and *imago dei*, as well as within the study of ethics, as in the book *Ethics* (1st Touchstone Edition, New York: Simon and Schuster, 1995) by Dietrich Bonhoeffer. A separate and helpful study would be to read the questions of difference and disability as we understand them back into the formulations of both Western and non-Western theologians. For the sake of brevity and focus, the current guide looks at writers from recent decades who directly address disability and theology to use their language in a way that feels accessible and directly applicable to current-day faith communities.

1. *What Does It Mean to Be a Person?*

A Theological Tension

A theological look at difference/disability demands that we hold two equally true realities in tension with each other: 1) difference and disability (in other words, human need and reliance) include all of us, with no exceptions; and 2) some people simply have much more difficult roads to follow, a fact that also must be respected.

If someone with normal mobility walks up to a house under construction, and workers haven't put in front steps yet, that person can't go into the house. It would take super-human strength to spring from the ground to an entryway that's some seven to ten feet above the ground. How do we deal with that? We put in steps. Which is all a way of saying that steps, which many people think of as a given, are in fact an accommodation. Steps are a support system, they're an assist for humans to get from one level to another. Admittedly, a larger number of people can use steps than can't, but that doesn't mean they're natural, that they're not a way to support and help humans who couldn't otherwise get somewhere without them. This basic example using something as everyday as brick or concrete steps helps us recognize the basic theological premise that we're all in this together.

In fact, in recent years a large midwestern university put in a system of ramps throughout the campus. Then in a follow-up survey, they asked people why they did it—not why they *should* put in ramps, but why they *did* put in ramps. The results were interesting. Those with strollers said it was done for them; delivery people with hand trucks said it was for them; people with wheelchairs saw it as being for them; and people who simply had a lot of stuff to carry saw it as making it safer for them. What the survey revealed was that once you put everyone on a level playing field, you realize that the boundaries we are used to thinking of are actually pretty artificial. Did the people pushing strollers have a handicap? Did the delivery people? Those in wheelchairs? Looked at from that perspective, the so-called handicap becomes not the limitation itself, but the value judgment we put on the limitation. We all have needs that call for different kinds of support.

Yet at the same time, we hold that universal need for help and support alongside the other theological premise: In the face of cultural and societal norms, some people simply have a harder row to hoe. That "difference," in turn, leads us to questions of suffering and theodicy and inexplicability.

For instance, someone may be aware of what she truly understands as her emotional disabilities, rooted in destructive childhood experiences, and part of who she has become as an adult. She's also aware that how she has learned to deal with those inner disabilities, through emotional supports and therapy, has become an important part of who she is and what she has to offer the world. At the same time, she is aware that she doesn't know what it's like to be, for example, the parent of a child with cerebral palsy, or to have cerebral palsy herself. And she lives with that tension, acknowledging her own, perhaps less visible, disabilities and need for support, while at the same time acknowledging that she can function within the norms of society more easily than some others can.

Terminology

The way we talk about difference and disability is a sensitive and complex area. Language has changed in recent years to reflect the idea that a disability isn't within someone; rather, it's where there is a disconnect happening between that person and his context. He may have something physical or cognitive that didn't develop typically, often called an impairment or an atypical development. But that only becomes a *dis*ability when the context he's in says he doesn't match up "right."

Take another everyday example: There's a paper towel dispenser in a public restroom made for someone who can reach six feet off the floor. As long as you can reach it, you have the ability to get the paper towel. Yet for someone shorter or in a wheelchair, a dispenser at that height might produce an inability, not so much because of the person but because of the placement of the dispenser. If the dispenser is placed lower, then there is no disconnect between the person in a wheelchair and the paper towel— hence, no "inability." The inability to reach has become an ability to reach.

How well we function is a product of what's available to us to meet our needs in our environment—even if it's just a paper towel. Yet when we look at it this way, what might seem like a minor adjustment in terminology actually ends up making a huge difference. To see the question of ability as linked to the space we're in doesn't let us pin the question of difference—and, thus, the fear that often comes with it—on the person with the difference or disability. Instead, those questions become about us. Or in biblical terms, as Jesus interacted with the blind man who then washed himself in the pool of Siloam, the sin is not in the person; sin is in how the world responds (John 9:1–7).

This applies to all of us. Think of the things such as supports, services, and networks that we've each needed to function, whether it was psychological or logistical support for something difficult or even debilitating. Think of the things and places inside of us that always seem disabled, atypical, or out of sync. It could be something as mundane as using reading glasses or learning another language, or something as extensive as regular therapy and support groups for an addiction, or a machine that helps someone who doesn't have use of her hands to type.

As we reflect on our lives in light of a broadened understanding of disability, our insights can extend to wounds we bear from our childhoods or other experiences that have caused us to need support and services to function effectively in the world. We all have those kinds of places inside of us. And we've probably all had occasions when other people were patient with and forgiving of our limitations, which lay right alongside our strengths.

As the saying goes, "We create ability by masking disability, and we create disability by masking ability."

To hold up the universal human condition of brokenness and need is not to trivialize disabilities that are more marked and that create more atypical challenges to get through life. But it is to broaden the theological circle to include all of us. And it affects, in turn, how we interact with and receive the ministry of people with more overt differences and disabilities. As the twentieth-century theologian Jurgan Moltmann wrote: "In actual fact, the distinction between the healthy and the handicapped does not exist. For every human life is limited, vulnerable, and weak. Helpless we are born and helpless we die. So in reality there is no such thing as a handicapped life. It is only the idea of health set up by the society of the capable which condemns a certain group of people to be called 'handicapped.'"[2]

How We as Christians Define Humanity

In light of this tension, what criteria then allow us to create the idea of a normative humanity, that is, our ability to say, "This is normal," or "This is not normal"? Though criteria such as autonomy, reason, and personal effectiveness have usually been seen as a given for any definition of normative humanity, a theology that sees differences and dependence as part of God and therefore part of the human condition prevents us from assuming those premises anymore.

Western culture has tended to define personhood by independence and rationality. It's a fundamental thread in classical theology, beginning with Tertullian and including Boethius in the sixth century: "A person is the individual substance of a rational nature." For subsequent Christian theologians, personhood often centered on the idea of individuality as something that's best expressed in feelings, words, and actions.

But certain differences and disabilities challenge these basic assumptions. If someone's individuality isn't as easily readable in their expression of words and feelings that others can understand, or actions that make sense to us, does that unconsciously challenge and upset our idea of what it is to be a person? Might that even be the reason some people are so uncomfortable around those with certain cognitive or communicative differences?

Yet maybe that discomfort is a good thing. Maybe it tells us that the assumed definition of personhood isn't one that gets us very far, and may even be something we all struggle with inside ourselves. A cultural emphasis on performance, achievement, and individuality is something we

---

2 Moltmann, *The Power of the Powerless*. San Francisco: Harper and Row, 1983, p. 137.

see the dangers of constantly, in how it contributes to stress, fear, self-rejection, a sense of scarcity, resentment and competition with others, and a lack of empathetic connection to those around us. It's those very qualities that faith communities often work hard to counter, trying instead to preach and emphasize a God whose love and mercy calls us to compassion, service, community—and vulnerability.

But maybe the church's effort to counter the social stereotypes of "what to do with your life," such as competing, gaining, winning, being in control of yourself and probably of others, needs to go even deeper to include countering the stereotype of what it means simply to be a person. What if the importance of clear and easily understood self-expression were inverted to say that our personhood is instead more about our acceptance of what we don't understand in the mystery of another person? Or what if the importance of personal autonomy and self-control were inverted to prioritize our dependence on others? Frankly, it is there, whether we want it to be or not. As Parker Palmer says, our lives are "two-footed intersections of people's lives." Why not go ahead and, as Christians, acknowledge that in our very definition of what it means to be a person?

Either one of those inversions would be a startling switch in our usual orientation, or either may not be complete on its own. But to think of such an inversion breaks up the ice floe of assuming individual humanity is defined by control, power, and easily understood self-expression. Do we need to rethink a definition of being human that leaves behind ideas like autonomy, self-definition, and power, and instead open ourselves—including opening our fears and hopes—to one that is about being in vulnerable, dependent relationship with others, in a community that sees that as part of its vision of the Trinity?

Loosening up the definition of what it is to be human also helps us avoid the danger of trying to normalize what it is to be a human based on what works in a social context. (For more, see *Vulnerable Communion: A Theology of Disability and Hospitality* by Thomas Reynolds and *Receiving the Gift of Friendship: Profound Disability, Theological Anthropology, and Ethics* by Hans Reinders.) Is what it is to be human a function of social usefulness or effectiveness, or social exchange—in other words, what we think of as essential to many of the relationships we engage in? Is it a certain "body capital," as Reynolds terms it, a physical resource and ability, from which any departure is seen as a problem? Is a definition of humanity some kind of idealized human integrity or human nature, whole and unbroken? As Christians who claim a God who was broken for the world, such a view of humanity would be inconsistent with that God. And would therefore undermine our saying that humanity was made in the image of God.

An expansive understanding of humanity would include even those who can't respond with "memory, reason, and skill," to quote the Episcopal Eucharistic Prayer C, or those who can't respond with agency or will, the very things we say God endowed us with. A reformed definition of humanity challenges our ways of thinking about how God intended us to be, at our core. What is it God sees and loves, versus how the world gauges being seen and loved? The longer we stay with that perspective, the more it can open up new vision for inclusive faith communities.

Indeed, shifting our definition of what it is to be a person helps us engage the inevitable reality that the question is not if, but when, disability touches our lives—for we are all participating in the aging process. "Again I saw that under the sun the race is not to the swift, nor the battle to the strong, nor bread to the wise, nor riches to the intelligent, nor favor to the skilful; but time and chance happen to them all. For no one can anticipate the time of disaster" (Ecclesiastes 9:11–12).

Talking about what's essential to being human also touches on what we really believe about resurrection. Is someone resurrected with the same body, with the same way of thinking, perceiving, or expressing? The same way of hearing and understanding others? How does disability work with the theology of the end times? As real as those questions might be to many of us, it's a mystery whose resolution we can't know but one that we can trust, in light of a loving God. As Paul would say, we don't know what resurrection will look like. "How are the dead raised? With what kind of body do they come?' Fool! What you sow does not come to life unless it dies . . . . The glory of the heavenly body is one thing, and that of the earthly is another" (1 Corinthians 15:35–36, 40). This side of the end times, we simply have to live in not knowing. For example, does heaven mean "no disability" or "no barriers"? Some people with disabilities ask not to be told they won't be "disabled," and say that they see their difference as part of who they are.

But for many, that's not a satisfying place to end up. So what we might be able to say further is that, in mystery, someone's heavenly body is what is glorious and loved about them, and based on biblical theology, there will not be suffering or limitation with that body. The gift nestled within that answer is in how it settles us, not in theoretical questions based on fear, but in the here-and-now of how God sees and loves, which will always thwart how we see and love.

Theodicy

Difference and disability can give rise to theodicy—in other words, to the questions of why, if God is both good and powerful as we claim, then how could a painful event, such as developmental disability, injury, or impairment, have happened. At their core, such questions are really—like so many of the psalms—a cry for a God that that person can believe in, a God they long for but feel they cannot see. Yet on a basic human level, those questions often end up feeling like, "Why me," or "Why my child?" Did God "do" this to teach us, to punish/reward us, or was God just letting things go on automatic pilot and isn't really involved here at all? How could God do this, or let this happen?

Painful questions like these have haunted humanity throughout history. The best answer is probably not a theoretical one but instead the hope for a loving, graceful, and suffering God who will guide us—and even shape our next questions. A pastor or teacher might say, "The God I know and understand wouldn't do this or uncaringly let it happen; how and why it happened is a mystery to me, too. But the God I know is with you in it, intimate and caring, each step of the way, and will find graces with you and for you."

It might be easier to think about a loving, suffering God who is with us in pain. But theodicy and difference/disability can also lead to more difficult questions about God the creator. For instance, did God create what seem to us to be disabilities? If we believe that everyone is somehow created in the image of God, then yes, all people are created in the divine image, including those who may have more atypical development. But the tender next step is not to project back onto God what might be human intentions and strategies for normalcy, which means taking care not to rely on the human assumptions that see a more extreme difference as "tragically negative" (Reynolds, p. 187). We can return to the idea of a disability not being something inherently wrong with someone, but as related more to that person's relationship to her context: "Disability is a factor of being finite and contingent in an open universe subject to elements of unpredictability, instability, and conflict" (Reynolds, p. 187). How any one of us is made in God's image is a mystery we're invited into, within a world that includes brokenness, dependence, and uncertainty.

2. *What Does It Mean to Be God?*

If we're made in God's image, it raises a double-sided question: Who are we—but also, who is God?

Who God is and what God looks like is one of the longest standing theological (meaning human) questions. And as humans, we've carved out bits of the answer, sometimes in ways that keep the question fluid and open to God's ongoing dialogue with us, and sometimes, sadly, in ways that close down the dialogue entirely. It's a sticky wicket for lots of reasons. How does gender work? Sexuality? God created both gender and sexuality, but are we to understand God as gendered or sexual in a human way? When we do, does it send us in the right direction? The old adage is useful, that "We're made in God's image, but we can't make God in our image."

When we ask who God is, it also gives rise to questions of things like rational ability, will, beauty, and power. We think of those things as both positive and desirable. Does that mean, then, that that is God's image? And that if someone doesn't seem to have those things, they are somehow less in God's image?

These are the tough questions asked by theologians such as Nancy L. Eiesland, Thomas E. Reynolds, and Hans S. Reinders: Does our own image of God *include* disability or difference? Does it have to be either/or? The crucified God was a disabled God, an unable God. The breaking of bread is about brokenness and being unwhole. The resurrected Christ still bore his wounds. Do those images help us lift the judgments we humans may usually place on inability, and on seeming "unwhole"?

Asking who God is also poses the question of relationship within the Trinity. We come down so often, especially these days in the church, to emphasizing interrelationship as key to the Trinity and to how we are to live in community as the Trinity lives in its community. There are several strands of classical theology that have focused on this over the centuries, including what it is to be separate and what it is to be giving, and on reciprocity and mutuality.

But if social relationship, and the ability to be separate and defined and to be in a highly mutual relationship with others, is what we're arriving at as core to the Trinity, then how does that feel for the parent of a child with autism or another social difference? Children with autism do have ways of showing social interaction, but at certain places on the autistic spectrum, or with diagnoses similar to autism, those may be harder to see at times. Parents may lose things like a sense of eye contact, of empathic response, of reciprocity, and even sometimes of the child's ability to say "I love you." How does that challenge a view of humanity that's based on an interactive, reciprocating Trinity? For those parents and children, how can we make them feel like they do not fall outside of the most basic theological premises of Trinitarian Christianity? That process may return us to understanding how a child with a social processing difference does indeed interact, understand, and self-express, only in ways that are probably not average. The gift to us all is that such a child gives us the chance to make our theological thinking grounded and real, rather than theoretical and disconnected to life, which can help make God more real, not less real.

Another key piece of the theological puzzle is the idea of a personal relationship with God. Although this sounds like more late twentieth-century language, it isn't. Thomas Aquinas addressed these issues of how we are capable of relationship with God based on what we can deduce about God. When a parent of a kid who has a different kind of social processing hears, "You have to have a personal relationship with Jesus," does it raise anxiety about that child's relationship with anyone, let alone someone they can't actually see? This provides us an opportunity to look more openly at how God works in all our relationships and gets us to explore in ways that don't leave out social and processing differences. That includes all of us, even when we're feeling a disconnection with all of those around us and with God. Bringing explanations about God to complex and often unclear human relationships also keeps us from getting too bumper sticker in our theology. That's another great gift from those with more marked differences: They don't let us get too cute about God.

Other strands of thinking about who God is include whether God is perfect and whether that means God can suffer. The suffering God is a salient line of thought in twentieth-century theology, especially between and after the world wars. Writings such as those by Dietrich Bonhoeffer open up God's power in powerlessness and suffering, "Only the suffering God can help." We began to rely more on the idea that the omnipotent one isn't a distant puppeteer but chooses to stand alongside the powerless, a perspective that brings us closer to liberation theology (for more, see Eiesland's *The Disabled God: Toward a Liberatory Theology of Disability*). That circle would include all of us at places in our lives, especially powerless places in our inner lives. But a shift toward liberation theology would also apply to those with difference and disability who have been less powerful in our culture and our church. Suffering isn't equal to disability, but the two often coincide. People with disabilities may often say, "I may not suffer very much from my disability, but I do from attitudes and barriers."

The way Aquinas handles it is by saying that God doesn't act in the world through direct action but through secondary causes. "Suffering and pain are not to be ascribed to the direct action of God but to the fragility and frailty of the secondary causes through which God works." So God didn't cause a disability, but will work through that fragility.

In more recent and concrete language, Reynolds sets up how he believes "traces of God's presence are woven into human experiences, as an elemental part of our existence." Again, he inverts the usual social dynamics, seeing God's presence as:

1. Gratitude—for existence as gift
2. Hope—for relationship beyond tragedy
3. The sense of God—for an extraordinary possibility in vulnerable ordinariness

Evidence of who God is works itself into our lives in those ways, offering confirmation of a vulnerable God—and thus, being made in God's image, of vulnerability as in the forefront of being human rather than a regrettable secondary by-product meant to be avoided.

In sum, theological thought around what it means to be God in light of difference and disability calls us to an ever-expanding affirmation of the value of each person—in other words, to the kind of Christian love known as agape love. This theology, and its broader view of love, challenges our need to create relative social value for each person, instead of absolute value of all people.

3. *Who Are God's People?*

Asking what it means to be human and what it means to be God leads to the third piece of the holy triangle. What does it mean to be "us"? In short, and in a constant challenge to human nature, it means to be *us*—and not *us* and *them*. Which, in turn, brings us to a new and deeper reliance on the basic moral premise of hospitality in a radical way.

Communities are how we show and experience belonging. Again underlining the ultimate and most important human message we can give children with learning differences is that of simply and unquestioningly belonging.

If vulnerability is what defines community—again, an inversion of the way power is usually seen in community—then Reynolds says it becomes essential to protect vulnerability against exploitation. If you name vulnerability as important, then you have to treat it as important. A society has to restructure its gear for that, which would result in a different way of looking at our social and legal structures and health-care structures, and probably, therefore, our church structures.

In particular, community with people with more marked differences and disability calls forth both visible and invisible disabilities in all of us and helps us move beyond the definitions of personhood such as power and achievement that can entrap all of us. Once again, the question ultimately becomes not one of medical condition and differences, but of diversity.

Shared community and acknowledgment that we all need support and that we all have limitations help each one of us accept and even embrace how those very disabilities, and how we've come to adapt to them, are part of making us who we are.[3]

An inverted view of humanity leads to an inverted and renewed understanding of community. As Palmer points out, our survival depends on community, as the deepest truth of our lives. Whether we acknowledge it or not, community is the reality in which we're grounded. It's not a goal to be achieved, but a gift to be received and a truth to which we must open ourselves.

The trick—and the gift—of including those with learning differences in faith communities is that such inclusion isn't ultimately achieved through strategies and techniques. First and foremost, it's a reality we simply need to be vulnerable to and appreciative of. As Palmer notes, we live in a world that's better at dividing than uniting. So we need to be open to being put back together, probably in ways we didn't foresee and that aren't always comfortable for us.

It's why the categories and terminology that we use in talking about learning differences are ultimately only of limited use, because they create, by definition, insiders and outsiders. That's not to say we shouldn't use them at a certain point along the way. Especially as diagnoses, they can be very helpful to a family in naming and understanding a child's difference and in getting appropriate support for it. A diagnosis can also help people, especially parents, realize that a disability isn't equal to the child. But basically, most people (and most parents, for their children) want understanding and acceptance simply as humans. It's why we, in faith communities, should begin and end somewhere other than the categories. Needs create services; gifts create communities.

Hospitality

Where we begin and end is hospitality; it's fundamental to community. Hospitality is a core value in the Old Testament, far more than many people realize. Rather than being delegated to thank-you notes or the feminine sphere, as has often been the case in more contemporary culture, it was a basic aspect of household and indeed male honor, integrity, and relationship with God. It was valuable not as an end in itself but because of what it points us back to: the basic biblical premise of opening ourselves up to be changed by another—especially someone who seems strange to us.

---

3 Drawing on Palmer, Parker. *"The Company of Strangers,"* Rochester, NY, 1988.

Indeed, in this way, there is self-interest in hospitality. We are all strangers to ourselves, not just to others. Parts of us are always strange to ourselves, in a way that eludes complete resolution. We all have those parts and can even end up "dismembering" ourselves internally by not accepting and loving them. What would happen if, in welcoming what made us uncomfortable in another person, we went a little further in embracing what makes us uncomfortable in ourselves?

Indeed, as Palmer points out, that may be why it's so difficult to truly include people with differences and disabilities in a radical hospitality. Because these "strangers," even if they're children or teens with different ways of learning and expressing themselves, reveal and challenge our illusions and the fears deep inside us that make those illusions necessary. These children—or rather our reactions to them—show our own spiritual poverty, how we're not really stoked up, or maybe at best only propped up, and oftentimes we don't want to deal with that. The paradox is that we often feel "disabled" about how to relate to people with disabilities.

In this way, the folks who elicit our reactions of fear and rejection are doing us a kind of favor, even if it doesn't feel like it. They're giving us a chance to become un-illusioned and to accept ourselves in a more real way, a more trustworthy way that includes more of each of us. In short, working with people who are different from us—in this case, children and teens who seem unusual and unable to "fit in"—helps us put ourselves back together. The gift ends up being one of healing and wholeness to the entire community.

Ultimately, as Palmer shows, people with disabilities puncture holes in all our comfortable illusions about both hospitality and our own disabilities:

1. The illusion that we know ourselves. Other people can call up the parts of us we don't know or are frightened of, the parts that contradict our need to see ourselves as in control and successful. We might choose at first to project those fears out onto the other and make it their problem, and then we have to go through a process of owning and accepting that part as ours, and as loveable. To love someone with a difference that frustrates us, or a disability that even frightens us, helps us love the disabled parts of ourselves—parts we have probably stigmatized unknowingly and possibly over many years. A clear learning difference in a child can evoke our fear of vulnerability and shame, or even those feelings themselves. Feeling like "I don't want your world" is really "I don't want those parts

of my own world." There's a gift and potential freedom in understanding that.

2. The illusion that we can know what goes on in another person. We can't, but with some folks we may be able to convince ourselves of that temporarily. More marked differences or disabilities in our own selves or others make us acknowledge the mystery of personhood and stop pretending that we can explain it or make ultimate sense of it.

3. Strangers puncture the illusion that we can alter reality to fit our image of how things should be, in other words, our obsession to fix. No wonder church members give up on "working with" a child or teen with a learning difference if their unconscious goal is to fix them to make it all look normalized. From the perspective of the child, it can be discouraging to have someone try to "save" you, which children can pick up on from a young age. So we're forced into the ministry of presence, of compassion and "being with," which is the only real ministry any of us can offer. It can look more or less obvious than that, but that's what it is at its core.

4. The illusion that we must earn love, belonging, and justification through our personal effort and clear results. Indeed, that's probably the internal disability that is closest to most of us: earning love by making things work, by keeping people from getting upset, by looking good, and by keeping things running smoothly. The child with a developmental learning difference who doesn't get results on our terms challenges this old experience of love. The child instead gives us the chance to replace it with a more graceful one within ourselves.

5. The cultural illusion that we'll avoid physical diminishment and death. As Jurgen Moltmann (*The Power of the Powerless*, p. 137–154) wrote, "We come into the world weak and helpless and we go out weak and helpless, and it's an illusion that we're anything else in between."

For each of us, confronting these illusions becomes a journey of deep and ongoing spiritual formation. That's one of many ways children and teens with learning differences can affect and change an entire faith community.

Theology As Lived in Your Community

Kids with learning differences don't let us linger too long on the idea of love in the abstract. Love becomes embodied, tangible, and grounded. They help us understand that the question isn't where people belong, but whom they belong to—not location but relationship. If they belong to God, then they belong to this community of the church.

They help us wrestle with a culture of forgiveness. Can you forgive me for my not understanding where you're really coming from and for not seeing your strengths? Can you forgive me for projecting my own fears onto you, and saying the wrong thing? Can I forgive you for the fear you bring up in me?

Within that forgiveness, parents of kids with learning differences will probably need some measure of absolution somewhere in the mix, either implicitly or explicitly. Culture still tends to blame parents, and even if the parents are educated and "know better," they may well carry a sense of guilt and fear that they did something wrong. At some moment when they're able to name their fears, they may need to experience the grace of absolution.

Such families may also need to experience the grace of abundance. In our culture, there's an ethos of gaining for one's self and of fighting for resources. For families who need extra support, especially those with financial strains that exist on all kinds of support networks, the church needs to feel like a place to experience abundance, whatever emotional, logistical, or spiritual form that might take. In this way, many families may come to know Christian hope and healing best through the experience of the community itself—through hospitality, accepting the stranger, learning, kindness, and being joyful. It may be the best embodiment of theology.

Nearly all the theology in the Bible is learned from stories. Even something as seemingly explicit as the Decalogue must be understood in the context of God's care for the Israelite community and God's deep desire for ongoing relationship. So too must our theology be understood in stories. Ask people for their story, and then let your stories become shared.

As your congregation includes children and adults with learning differences and disabilities, there will be moments and experiences that create great stories. Ask any group of parents or adults with disabilities to tell you their faith stories, and you'll get stories full of preaching and transformative possibilities. The challenge and the grace in faith communities is for my story and your story to become our story—and an ongoing part of *God's* story.

Selective Bibliography

❖

Anderson, Bruce. *Our Door Is Open: Creating Welcoming Cultures in Helping Organizations*. CD. Vashon, WA: Community Activators, 2010. http://www.communityactivators.com/home/our-door

Ariel, Cindy, and Robert A. Naseef, eds. *Voices From the Spectrum: Parents, Grandparents, Siblings, People with Autism, and Professionals Share Their Wisdom*. Philadelphia: Jessica Kingsley Publishers, 2006.

Barone, John, and the Monarch School. *A Place for All: Ministry for Youth with Special Needs*. Winona, MN: St. Mary's Press, 2008.

Betcher, Sharon V. *Spirit and the Politics of Disablement*. Minneapolis: Fortress Press, 2007.

Block, Jennie Weiss. *Copious Hosting: A Theology of Access for People with Disabilities*. New York: Continuum, 2002.

Bolt, Sarah. *Your Feet, My Shoes: Activities to Help Children in Grades 1–8 Understand and Include Peers with Disabilities*. Wyoming, MI: Christian Learning Center [CLC] Network, 2009.

Breeding, Hood, et al. *Let All the Children Come to Me: A Practical Guide to Including Children with Disabilities in Your Church Ministries*. Colorado Springs, CO: Cook Communications, 2006.

Carter, Erik W. *Including People with Disabilities in Faith Communities: A Guide for Service Providers, Families, and Congregations*. Baltimore: Paul Brookes Publishing, 2007.

Creamer, Debbie Beth. *Disability and Christian Theology: Embodied Limits and Constructive Possibilities*. New York: Oxford University Press, 2009.

Dimensions of Faith and Congregational Ministries with Persons with Developmental Disabilities and Their Families: A Bibliography and Address Listing of Resources for Clergy, Laypersons, Families, and Service Providers. New Brunswick, NJ: Elizabeth M. Boggs Center on Developmental Disabilities, Robert Wood Johnson School, 2009. http://rwjms.umdnj.edu/boggscenter

Eiesland, Nancy L. *The Disabled God: Toward a Liberatory Theology of Disability.* Nashville: Abington Press, 1994.

Gaventa, W., and W. Berk. Brain Injury: *When the Call Comes—A Congregational Resource.* New Brunswick, NJ: The Boggs Center, Brain Injury Association of New Jersey, and New Brunswick Theological Seminary, 2001.

Gillibrand, John. *Disabled Church—Disabled Society: The Implications of Autism for Philosophy, Theology, and Politics.* Foreword by Dr. Rowan Williams. Philadelphia: Jessica Kingsley Publishers, 2010.

Groome, Thomas H. *Sharing Faith: A Comprehensive Approach to Religious Education and Pastoral Ministry.* Eugene, OR: Wipf and Stock, 1998.

Hauerwas, Stanley, and Jean Vanier. *Living Gently in a Violent World: The Prophetic Witness of Weakness.* Chicago: InterVarsity Press, 2008.

Hubach, S. and Joni Eareckson Tada. *Same Lake, Different Boat: Coming Alongside People Touched by Disability.* Phillipsburg, NJ: P&R Publishing, 2006.

Keely, Robert J., ed. *Shaped by God: 12 Essentials for Nurturing Faith in Children, Youth, and Adults.* Grand Rapids: Faith Alive Christian Resources, 2010.

Kluth, Paula. *You're Going to Love This Kid!: Teaching Students with Autism in the Inclusive Classroom.* Baltimore: Brookes Publishing Company, 2003.

Le Fevre, Dale N. *Best New Games: 77 Games and 7 Trust Activities for All Ages and Abilities.* Champaign, IL: Human Kinetics, 2002.

Luurtsema, Kimberly S. and Barbara J. Newman. *G.L.U.E. training manual* (Giving Loving Understanding Encouraging). Wyoming, MI: Christian Learning Center [CLC] Network, 2009.

Naseef, Robert A. *Special Children, Challenged Parents: The Struggles and Rewards of Raising a Child with a Disability.* Baltimore: Paul Brookes Publishing, 2001.

Newman, Barbara. *Autism and Your Church: Nurturing the Spiritual Growth of People with Autism Spectrum Disorders.* Grand Rapids: Faith Alive Christian Resources, 2006.

_____. *Body Building: Devotions to Celebrate Inclusive Community.* Wyoming, MI: Christian Learning Center [CLC] Network, 2009.

_____. *Helping Kids Include Kids with Disabilities.* Grand Rapids: Faith Alive Christian Resources, 2001.

Palmer, Parker. "Merging Two Worlds." Keynote address called "The Company of Strangers," Rochester, NY, 1986 (available through the Elizabeth M. Boggs Center on Developmental Disabilities, UMDNJ-Robert Wood Johnson Medical School, 732-235-9304, http://rwjms.umdnj.edu/boggscenter)

Pearson, Sharon Ely. *Living IN-Formation*, monthly Christian Formation newsletter. New York: Church Publishing Incorporated. spearson@cpg.org.

Pierson, Jim, et al. *Special Needs, Special Ministry for Children's Ministry.* Loveland, CO: Group Publishing, 2004.

Preheim-Bartel, Dean A., Aldred H. Neufeldt, Paul D. Leichty, and Christine J. Guth. *Supportive Care in the Congregation: Providing a Congregational Network of Care for Persons with Significant Disabilities*, rev. ed. Scottdale, PA: Mennonite Publishing Network, 2011.

Rapada, Amy. *The Special Needs Ministry Handbook: A Church's Guide to Reaching Children with Disabilities and Their Families.* BookSurge Publishing, 2007.

Reinders, Hans S. *Receiving the Gift of Friendship: Profound Disability, Theological Anthropology, and Ethics.* Grand Rapids: Wm. B. Eerdmans Publishing, 2008.

_____, ed. *The Paradox of Disability: Responses to Jean Vanier and L'Arche Communities from Theology and the Sciences.* Grand Rapids: Wm. B. Eerdmans Publishing, 2010.

Reynolds, Thomas E. *Vulnerable Communion: A Theology of Disability and Hospitality.* Grand Rapids: Brazos Press, 2008.

Scanlan, Audrey, and Linda Snyder. *Rhythms of Grace: Worship and Faith Formation for Children and Families with Special Needs.* Harrisburg, PA: Morehouse Publishing, 2010.

Spellers, Stephanie. *Radical Welcome: Embracing God, the Other, and the Spirit of Transformation.* New York: Church Publishing, 2006.

Walsh, Mary Beth, Alice F. Walsh, and William C. Gaventa, eds. *Autism and Faith: A Journey into Community.* New Brunswich, NJ: The Elizabeth M. Boggs Center on Developmental Disabilities, Robert Wood Johnson Medical School, 2008, http://rwjms.umdnj.edu/boggscenter

Webb-Mitchell, Brett. *Beyond Accessibility: Toward Full Inclusion of People with Disabilities in Faith Communities.* New York: Church Publishing, 2010.

Vos Wezeman, Phyllis, and Anna L. Liechty. *Many Saints, Many Ways: Multiple Intelligences Activities for Grades 1 to 6.* Notre Dame, IN: Ave Maria Press, 2003.

Yong, Amos. *The Bible, Disability, and the Church: A New Vision of the People of God*. Grand Rapids: Wm. B. Eerdmans Publishing, 2011.

_____. *Theology and Down Syndrome: Reimagining Disability in Late Modernity*. Waco: TX: Baylor University Press, 2007.

Young, Frances M. *Brokenness and Blessing: Towards a Biblical Spirituality*. Grand Rapids: Baker Academic, 2007.

Online resources:

_____. *The 411 on Disability Disclosure: A Workbook for Youth with Disabilities*, http://www.ncwd-youth.info/411-on-disability-disclosure (Self-Advocacy)

Accessibility Guidelines for Episcopal Churches (2008) downloadable on the Episcopal Church Building Fund's website, http://www.ecbf.org/access.html

American Association on Intellectual and Developmental Disabilities, www.AAIDD.org

American Associate of People with Disabilities, http://www.aapd.com/site/c.pvI1IkNWJqE/b.5606969/k.7853/AAPD_Interfaith_Initiative.htm

Anabaptist Disabilities Network, http://www.adnetonline.org/

Children At Worship, http://www.childrenatworship.org/welcome.html

Council for Exceptional Children, http://www.cec.sped.org/am/template.cfm?section=Home

CLC [Christian Learning Center] Network, http://www.clcnetwork.org

The Elizabeth M. Boggs Center on Developmental Disabilities, New Brunswick, NJ, http://www.rwjms.umdnj.edu/boggscenter (See under Projects and Products)

Envision Access: 20 Ideas for Accessible Worship. Written transcript from webinar at http://www.laurelville.org/envision_access

Episcopal Disability Network, http://www.disability99.org

Friendship Ministries, http://www.friendship.org/

A Guide to the ADA Accessibility Guidelines for Play Areas (2005) United States Access Board, (800) 872-2253 (v); (800) 993-2822 (TTY), http://www.access-board.gov/play/guide/intro.htm

Homilies by E-mail, Sermon Resources, Worship Resources, E-Books, http://www.homiliesbyemail.com/leaf/activity-sheets.html

Jewish Community Inclusion Program for People with Disabilities, http://www.jfcsmpls.org/inclusionresources.html

Joni and Friends, http://www.joniandfriends.org/

National Catholic Partnership on Disability, http://www.ncpd.org/

National Council of Churches USA, Committee on Disabilities, http://www.ncccusa.org/nmu/mce/dis/

Index

❧